GLEANINGS

FROM

WESTERN PRAIRIES.

GLEANINGS

FROM

WESTERN PRAIRIES

BY THE

Rev. W. E. YOUNGMAN

BOOKS FOR LIBRARIES PRESS

FREEPORT, NEW YORK

First Published 1882
Reprinted 1971

INTERNATIONAL STANDARD BOOK NUMBER:
0-8369-5870-5

LIBRARY OF CONGRESS CATALOG CARD NUMBER:
72-161002

PRINTED IN THE UNITED STATES OF AMERICA

TO

The Rev. Charles William Giles, D.D.,

THE HALL, MILTON, NEAR CAMBRIDGE,

AS A UNITED THANK-OFFERING ON THE PART OF MANY AGED,

MANY SICK, AND MANY POOR FAMILIES

IN ENGLAND AND OTHER COUNTRIES, WHOSE FULL HEARTS

CAN MAKE HIM NO RETURN UPON EARTH,

BUT WHOSE PRAYERS ARE SWEET SUCCOUR WITHIN

"THE GOLDEN GATES."

Cambridge,
    July, 1882.

CONTENTS.

CHAPTER IX.

CHAPTER X.

CHAPTER XI.

CHAPTER XII.

CHAPTER XIII.

CHAPTER XIV.

CHAPTER XV.

CHAPTER XVI.

CHAPTER XVII.

CHAPTER XVIII.

CHAPTER XIX.

CHAPTER XX.

CHAPTER XXI.

CHAPTER XXII.

CHAPTER XXIII.

CHAPTER XXIV.

CHAPTER XXV.

CHAPTER XXVI.

CHAPTER XXVII.

PROLOGUE.

A VOLUME of simple word painting, an effort to sketch that far Western Prairie life, to lay it unglossed before you. Accept it as such, and you won't be disappointed, I hope, as scenes are grouped before you which happened in days and nights already sunk into Eternity.

It may be strange to invite you to that far frontier, and show you the life and ways of men who have gone forth from our own old world, drawn to that new world by that sole boon of man—*hope*. Yet *hope* does much for poor humanity. I think it was Carlyle who wrote of hope thus: "O blessed hope, sole boon of man, whereby on his strait prison walls are painted beautiful far-stretching landscapes, and into the night of very death is shed holiest dawn. Thou art to all an indefeasible possession in this God's world—to the wise a Constantine-like banner written on the eternal skies, under which they shall conquer, for the battle itself is victory: to the foolish some secular mirage, or shadow of still waters painted on the parched Earth, whereby at least their dusty pilgrimage, if devious, becomes cheerfuller, becomes possible."

A friend told me before I knew that Western life, " It's like a small drizzling rain wetting a man to the skin. Its *ennui* will soak into your soul." I don't agree with him now I know Western life, although at that time my friend's remark made me dread Western travel. If you, Reader, are as agreeably surprised as I was, we, as you close this volume, shall part good friends.

Should my poor thoughts awaken a nobler thrill of sympathy within you, and give you but a passing interest in that busy frontier, and that wild Indian world, so far distant yet close to our own, now that Steamers plough the strong waves of the Atlantic, and the Iron Road stretches onward to Indian Territory, my time will not have been vainly spent, the arrow will have flown to the target's heart.

To my Ecclesiastical Friends I would suggest the importance of giving some kind of recommendation to families leaving their parishes to the Clergy of the Country and district whither they are going. Many who are good Christians in Europe recede totally from their faith abroad, and in the heterogeneous mass of society they find on the frontier of the New World lead faithless and loveless lives.

And yet a kind word, or a friendly interest, might have made all so different.

I have to thank the great Indian missionary, the Rev. P. J. De Smet, S.J., for many of my notes on Indian life.

As I write my acknowledgements my memory carries me back (nigh nine years ago) to his one room in the Catholic University of St. Louis, Missouri. In memory's clear painting I still see that dear old man who for me will ever inhabit that cell as at our first interview. Everything connected with it is so vividly before me. The sun-light still seems to stream through the window over his face as it then did, goldening the white locks straying from under his Biretta. His own pet Mocking-Bird, with its quiet saucy ways perched upon his shoulder, the sleeve of his Soutane, or the peak of his Biretta, else resting lovingly upon his hand, as it did those years agone in his Convent cell. It is indeed a pleasure to remember the missionary De Smet, who with his own hand turned for me the pages of his manuscript notes, who showed and explained to me his sketches on Indian life, made roughly oft-times upon the Western Prairies. It is a pleasure to recall that voice unravelling what I, with my European ignorance, could not understand; and I have always treasured up his permission to make what notes I wished from his conversation, and the manuscripts lent me to peruse in my several visits to him.

A pioneer of the Western Prairies, a Traveller, a Geographer and a Scientist, his notes and maps relating to Indian Territory were valuable to the Government of the United States and his "Society." The grandest monument to him, is the one he unknowingly built for himself, in taking out to civilize that Western life nigh one hundred and ten Missionaries to the Province of Missouri.

I have not forgotten the sorrow that crept over me when one day going to the College to make enquiries about his illness, before seeing him the Brother Concierge told me, " He is dead." I remember standing by his open coffin in the Church of the University, and thoughts of those dim prairie wayfarings of his rushing over me. His dead hands even then were clasping the Chalice and Paten as though he were still pleading that awful Sacrifice, whilst that death smile upon his face seemed sadder than tears.

A sense of desolation looked out from many faces as the *cortége* left S. Louis for S. Stanilaus, Florissant, in whose little cemetery he rests in peace (I doubt not) with those other Angeli of the everlasting truth, his companions in warfare.

With grateful memory I linger over that bright day in Italy, when the late President of the Academy of Noble Ecclesiastics in Rome (Monsignore Odoardo Agnelli, Bishop of Troy, i.p.i.) spoke of my two former volumes to his late Holiness Pius the Ninth (of happy memory to us who saw him near). The words of His Holiness at that Audience will always remain with me—brave and strong words, bidding me always fight for the Truth.

I have to thank so many for the kindness with which my two former volumes were received in the New World. His Eminence the Cardinal Archbishop of New York, for his personal censorship of the Theological Treatise in my former volume ("For Husks, Food"); also their Graces the Archbishops Purcell (of Cincinnati) and Kendrick (of St. Louis), for their kindly written words of congratulation ; also His Grace Archbishop Corrigan (of New York) for his encouraging letter written from Seton Hall during the time of his Episcopate in Newark. To both clergy and laity of the New and Old Worlds, who then wrote me words of kindness I, as though personally. to each one, tender grateful thanks. Many of these letters I have sorted, and keep in an Album peculiar to them.

Special thanks I owe to one Parish Priest of New York for his help in manuscript revision, and to the *then* Provincial of "the Society" in Maryland for his honest critique, which I much value, and shall always wish to profit by.

CHAPTER I.

"I might have striven, and striven in vain
  Such visions to recall,
Well known and yet forgotten: now
  I see, I hear them all.
The present pales before the past,
  Who comes with angels' wings,
As in a dream I stand, amidst
  Strange yet familiar things."—*Proctor*.

THE RANCHER'S HOME.

WO men are journeying over the prairie in a light waggon from the Osage Mission in Neosho County, Kansas, to a Rancher's home.

A Rancher's home, on the broad prairie.

One fresh from the scenes of European capitals, the other well seasoned to the strange silence of that prairie life.

Have you seen the prairie? watched the sheeny sunlight flood with strange beauty that long stretch of view, over which the eyes wander wonderingly? felt European trammels shaken from your soul by that still, primitive life? lost yourself in wonderment as the immensity of country grew upon you? Have you travelled over those

1

vast tracts of prairie land, whose very vastness causes one to recognise the pigmyism, the littleness of self, aye, causes even the smallness of Europe to enter with a distinct forcibility into the soul?

Have you gazed over the prairies during the Indian summer, joyed in that one field of vast verdure, enamelled with bright odoriferous wild flowers, whose brilliant beauty has few other witnesses than the azure firmament?

Have you scanned one by one its undulations, been borne as it were from wave to wave, from valley to hilltop, as you found yourself in that limitless plain?

The prairie, and the Indian summer, with its clear sunlight, its myriad wild flowers growing everywhere around that prairie home, could only have tempted one of those travellers to make trial of a Rancher's home, and stay those months in the " Far West " whither his friend had invited him.

It is a strange feeling to labor under at first, the knowledge that there is only the distance of thirty miles between yourself and the scalping knife; yet it is on the frontier formed by that band of whites who have no fears of Indians (thanks to the missioners), that the events you are about reading happened. Judge yourselves if that strange life is worth the living.

Willie Woodhouse was lost in reverie, and his friend the Rancher was watching him from his seat in the light waggon. The smoke curled lazily from the Rancher's pipe, and the tired horses stooped their heads to drink

at the prairie creek. Charles Kirwan the Rancher turned
and touched his companion with the rein to awaken him
from his reverie.

He started ; had he been day-dreaming only a few
minutes ?

"Well, old fellow, what do you think of this country,
eh ?"

It was a middle-aged man, perhaps thirty-five, who
spoke, a pleasant ring his voice had then, and the sun-
light shimmered over his dark beard and his well-cut
features, lightening the dark hair showing under the
Rancher's cap.

The Rancher's guest was in no dreamland—all was
reality—but such a pleasant reality that afternoon in
the hazy Indian summer.

They had skirted along one side of the prairie, and
were about to cross the creek ("crick," the settlers called
it). These creeks are small streams of water running
through the prairies, and on the banks of such streams
a belt of trees is always to be found. They had pene-
trated into one of these belts of trees, and were by the
side of the stream, about to cross over.

Woodhouse, sitting on the side of the waggon, with
his eyes turned to the prairies, had not perceived this
until his friend spoke, and it is at this entrance to the
prairie life I present to my readers Charles Kirwan, a
self-made man.

I don't know if you would call him handsome. He
had a winning smile on his lips, and his expression

changed with the thoughts that passed through his brain. All beauty he claimed rested in his expression, which lit up those otherwise too regular features with a strange fire, and then his soul shone forth indeed.

Yes, he had a great soul, and gloried in his prairie isolation and his prairie home.

But of his dark moments—and we all have dark moments in our lives—then his features were a very fear.

Of middle height, lithe as a leopard, and full of mirth, one would have had no fear of *ennui* in the visit to the Prairie Cattle Ranche.

The touch of his rein upon his guest's hand had recalled him to the present.

"Are you surprised at the extent of our prairie," he said, and a laugh broke forth from his lips as he pointed to the bank opposite. "You will be more surprised to cross that stream?"

The creek had been originally a run hollowed out by the tread of many thousand buffaloes, and sure enough the bank opposite was the steepest piece of track he had seen for a waggon to go up, even in the mountain roads of Europe.

"We can never do it, Charley."

How he laughed at his surprise. "Never do it! my horses and I often go over there. I think sometimes they could crawl up the wall of a house ; they beat the Tivoli mules for that. Well, we will let them rest for a few minutes longer. We have five miles in the prairie to go before we get to Walnut Creek. I am waiting to see your surprise at my home on the prairies. No luxurious Langham Hotel in Portland Place. A mud hut? No! well, not quite that. A tree shanty lined with mortar—a cooking stove, a fire-place, shelves for grocery, and a few plates. A loft for my two boys and the man, a lean-to—our bedroom that—a rough plank bedstead, a tin basin to wash in, four inches of looking glass. Can you stand it, eh, friend Englishman?"

"I think so. I have come some hundreds of miles from New York to try."

"Good. And for tho bright side—d'ye see that box in the waggon?"

Woodhouse nodded.

" I have sheets there. Your European body couldn't rest in blankets as mine does."

"I don't know that."

"Well, well. You will have a horse to ride, the great prairie for your course. You will see such sunrises and sunsets as only Kansas prairies boast. Color! talk of color, I have seen the rich purples fade into crimson, and one great bank of crimson fade again to all shades of its own color, intermixed with gold, and then whilst I looked it was night and darkness, and god-like, quiet even from the insects' myriad voices near me."

"Did you always love the prairies thus?"

"Yes; partly for gain, partly for æsthetics. My ranche is dearer to me than all the luxury of European life. When I travelled and met you in Europe, I wanted to see what men call the great, and grand, and beautiful,

in the cities of Italy, Germany, France, and England;
but I came back to my prairie life, as the caged bird
does to its freedom. I am happier here."

" Shall I be so ?"

" I can't tell. We are rough—my men and table,
and house rougher. If you are what I take you to be
you will conquer your prejudices, and the time you pass
here will be the happiest of your life."

" If I am not what you take me to be ?"

" Then you have always the train that stops at the
Mission ; you can return to your boasted civilization.
But we must be going ; night falls quickly during
the Indian summer, and we might lose the track."

It was all so pleasant by the side of the creek ; lithe
rabbits sunning themselves, and frisking by their warren ;
bright birds moving amongst the branches of the trees,
and the woodpecker's bill tapping upon the tree trunks
being the only audible sound, excepting the hum of
insects, and their own (to them) interesting chat.

" Will you take one of the horses and ride over the
creek, and then I will fetch the waggon ?"

" No, Charley, let's go together."

And so they went. The water was high up the horses'
knees, over the axle of the waggon wheels, and then
they were mounting the perilous bank. Twice they
essayed, and then, after such a piece of steep path as
a European would have imagined horses could never
surmount, with one of Charley's ringing cheers they
were on the prairie once more.

Woodhouse felt he was very pale, and yet he thought he had hardiesse in his character.

Once more the sheeny sun-light flooded the vast prairie, whilst here and there he saw low one-roomed cottages standing out on their claims, with the patch of corn-land close by, a would-be peach orchard now and again showing itself as an isolated sign of civilization.

"Do you see," said Kirwan, "that brown speck in the distance yonder?"

Woodhouse looked in the direction he pointed too with his whip, and there sure enough as the distance lessened he made out the Rancher's home.

His heart sank below zero. Had he travelled so many miles for this—to stay in this cottage? Why, his father's groom in Old England would have scorned such a shanty as this Kansas ranche. He had no such cottage on his place. And yet Charley Kirwan, the rich rancher, lived here.

On and on trotted the horses, nearer and nearer he drew to his fate. In a scope of hundreds of miles the only man he knew was Charley Kirwan.

He looked ruefully at his trunk full of books and European luxuries. What good could they be in such a cottage as this?

And yet the memory of his books consoled him, and the sight of a great purple sunset glory flooding and making beautiful the outside of the ranche reconciled him to his fate, for he dearly loved æsthetics.

There was a kind of romance, too, in the situation, and after all he would try it.

Charley Kirwan knew what was passing in his mind, for he smiled one of his knowing smiles.

" Cheer up, my friend ; Kansas life will do you more good than all your European travel, and as for experience, you will gain more here than elsewhere."

Reader, judge for yourself in closing this volume, was he right ?

The waggon stopped in the full glory of the sunset, as the gleamy light fell over the hut, beautifying even the external ugliness of the structure.

" Cottage," had he called it ? that word slipped from his vocabulary for ever when he had seen it.

" Tom,—Tom,—Tom," roared Charley Kirwan.

The door opened, and Tom issued forth.

Tom, in rough knee boots, knee breeches, and a cloth shirt.

Tom leered at Woodhouse, leered at his clothes, leered at the large box, leered at the valise, and with supreme contempt assisted in carrying them to the lean-to.

And the lean-to had no glass in the four-paned window for days after their arrival. They hung some sacking over that, so that the place was sleepable in after all.

" Tom, this is the gentleman we were expecting."

Tom scratched his head, eyed him from head to foot, walked round him, and held out his hand.

The guest felt almost ashamed of his hand near that other large, horny, brown hand, one so much younger and stronger than the other. Tom regarded that hand with wonder, and then said :

"I'll try and teach yer to like it ; but yer not broke in yet, that's sure."

From that time Tom and Woodhouse were fast friends.

Whilst this scene was going on Woodhouse had caught a glimpse of the inside of the ranche.

As Charley said, there it was—the rough floor, the stone hearth, on which a wood fire was blazing : an American cooking stove standing out in the room, a table covered with oilcloth, the shelves for grocery and plates, a lamp, and a few rough chairs. In one corner a ladder leading up to the loft. All this shut in 20 feet by 15 feet.

The bed-room, the lean-to. Woodhouse noticed the two-inch chinks where it joined on to the building proper. A rough bedstead indeed there ; the wood composing it not even planed by the maker; the tin wash-basin, the four-inch looking-glass, all perfectly as Charley had said.

This was to be his home for some months, and what events those months shut in ! as dissolving views, the chapters of this volume will pass before you.

Happy days, streaked with sunshine and quietude, over-ridden ofttimes by the grim shadow of pain and death ; yet days he thanked Providence for, and whose memory he loved in after years.

In the meanwhile Jack, another ranche boy, had prepared the evening meal, and they sat down to pork chops, prairie chicken, corn bread, stewed peaches and coffee, as soon as they entered.

So soon after that sunset it was night. No long gloaming as in England. The lamp was lit, and the blinds drawn down, and with appetites only such as prairie air could create, they did full justice to the plenteous fare. Slice after slice of luscious hot corn bread disappeared, cup after cup of coffee.

Charley Kirwan in his quiet way had drawn out the conversation with the boys who sat with them on their work on the farm, and about the cattle ; and Woodhouse, interested by the very strangeness of the scene, entered into it with his whole heart.

He had no idea how time flew until they pulled out their watches, and Charley Kirwan laughed that still laugh of his as he asked his guest to pull round by the fire and smoke, as every one in the ranche would be moving early next morning.

"Breakfast at 6.30 or 7. We are up soon after four, you know."

Then they made the beds. Those precious sheets were pulled out of the box, to the amusement of the two boys, who vowed it was the funniest move possible.

"And how are we to make the bed, Charley ?" they asked. (Here all distinction between master and servant was at an end.) "How do these things go ?"

How they laughed ; and how quickly that dreaded first evening had flown ; so pleasantly too, that the stranger regretted it had come to an end.

On that first evening he too thought his trunk out of place in the Rancher's home, as he took from it those necessaries he required.

Could it be he was about to sleep in a ranche on the wide prairies of the " Far West ?" that he was in Kansas ? Was he dreaming ? No ; the loud snoring of the ranche boys from their loft told him plainly it was reality.

CHAPTER II.

"The present hour repeats upon its strings
　　Echoes of some vague dream we have forgot;
Dim voices whisper half remembered things,
　　And when we pause to listen, answer not."—
　　　　　　　　　　A. B. Proctor.

PRAIRIE LIFE.—BROWN KIRWAN.

THE ranche door flung wide open on the following morning, and the bright sunshine flooding the interior of the building shows us Willie Woodhouse busily engaged in brushing some of the dirt and dust from the common sitting room of the ranche.

Then he cleaned the windows, washed up the breakfast things, and sat down with his books before him.

Charley Kirwan and his helpers had left him alone hours ago.

From door and window the sweet scent of prairie flowers crept into the rough building, the sunshine throwing into bold relief the shadows.

The tongues of fire flickered and curled around, and through the crevices of the heavy logs piled upon the hearth, and made beautiful the soft white wood ashes round ; as they lay piled up in the great recess, where the sun could not reach, did it try ever so hard.

The susurra of the prairie wind in amongst the Indian corn patch was real music.

Willie Woodhouse did not move from his books ; they were on prairies and prairie life, and he would know something of this before he essayed exploring the country round, and he had also promised Charley Kirwan to wait in for his brother, Brown Kirwan.

It was ten o'clock in the morning, but in the still prairie life that was late in the day to those who rose with the sunshine, and retired an hour or so after darkness had fallen.

A strong shadow fell over his book, and a voice, with an unmistakeable Dutch accentuation close by, woke him from his studies.

It was Herr Lieboldt, the head farmer of Charley Kirwan.

"Ee-ee-ee. Sharley say him frind am cum, eee-eee-eee. What hands, ee-ee ! What ed, ee-ee-ee ! Wat buk am you read ? I Lieboldt. I ed man. Me frind ob Sharley also, ee-ee. What tink you ob Sharley's home ? "

Short, red-haired, thick-set, Lieboldt, with his sharp blue eyes twinkling under rugged brows, was a character of whom Kirwan knew the full value.

"You cum see me ? My ole voman, ee-ee, be glad to see you. You see my house, my mule, my boys, ee-ee."

"Where am Sharley ?" Receiving an answer, this intruder departed, to be followed by a tall thin man, whose lantern jaws and sad eyes spoke of misery. Levett his name, real nasal American his twang. "So you've come, eh ? Well, where's Sharley ? I want to borrer a cup of coffee ; I can't go to the Mission to get none. I'll take the coffee. Good-bye, man." And he took the coffee and absconded, to the amazement of his auditor. Next came a Canadian-looking woman, short, thin, and age as difficult to tell as to guess the extent of prairie near. "Where's Sharley, eh, my man ?" she said. "I want to borrow a cup of coffee kernels ; he'll let me have it if he's at home. Not to home ! well, I guess I'll take it ; tell him I'll bring it back to-morrow." (Her to-morrows were long far-off days that never came.) As she said the "to-morrow" a smile flitted over her face at the greenness of Kirwan's guest in letting her have what she wanted.

"If yer want washing done, I'm yer woman to do it, I guess. Good bye ; don't forget to tell Sharley. I guess you will, though."

"Are these my neighbours and friends ?" soliloquised Woodhouse. "What can I do for them in these months to come ?" "Wait and see. God will use you if He wants you." It was a kind, gentle voice that spoke, the owner of the voice sitting in a spider buggy, driven close over the soft turf up to the window, and he sat looking in. It was Brown Kirwan, whose approach had hurried off the Canadian woman, who not only contemplated sugar, but coffee also. He had caught some of the conversation, and was smiling at it, mentally resolving to chaff Woodhouse about his greenness in allowing himself to be thus entreated by the ranchers near.

"I'm Brown Kirwan. You are Willie Woodhouse, Charley's friend. Will you be mine too?" They shook hands heartily, and then Brown descended from his buggy, took a chair, and sat in the bright sunlight in the ranche door.

"Let's have something to eat, and then you will come for a drive with me. I'm going to see a sick squatter's wife who is half Indian—about two miles away."

Brown Kirwan was a doctor living at the Osage Mission. He was tall, pale, with dark black hair, features more irregular than those of his brother, yet he had a kindly nature, and a heart as true as ever beat in human breast. He had served as surgeon in some regiment during the war between North and South, made a respectable little fortune, bought a claim out West, and started a sheep ranche. Perhaps he had been unsuccessful; certain it is, he had rented his claim to another, and taken again to his profession amongst the many squatters, and the small town forming round the Mission House of the Jesuits amongst the Osages.

Such was Brown Kirwan; a man full of knowledge, less picked up from books than knowledge practical, caught up in the hard run of daily life. His religion was founded and rooted in charity.

He seldom went to a church; but, as he often said, his church was the boundless prairie, the roof the blue curtain of heaven. There prayer welled out of his heart silently and naturally, as the sururra passing over the prairie grass, or the water welling up from the almost hidden spring near the ranche he once inhabited.

"But what has Charley to eat before we go, eh? Corn bread, I see. Good. And a lot of stewed peaches," as he lifted the lid off a saucepan standing on a form.

Good again. Also beans cooked in pork grease. Come on, friend, we shall be hungry before we return."

So they feasted, with no set table, on the good things there, and then mounting together in the buggy after locking the ranche door, drove off.

The drive was over the prairie grass to the side of a distant creek some miles off. The air was odorous with the Indian summer flowers, the atmosphere clearer even than in Italy (though unsung, and generally unknown to be so), and the enlivening conversation of Brown Kirwan made that first day on the prairies enjoyable to his companion.

"You are English, Mr. Woodhouse." "Yes." "What age? Well, never mind; I can see, from nineteen to twenty-two. Ah, you have life before you. I am double your age now. Well, I shouldn't wish to live my life over again. Dear me, your English life must be different to this. Your pale skin will soon gain American olive."

"My brother Charley is a Catholic. Dear me; well, he knows best. He worships God his way, I mine. You're of his religion. Well, well; more to interest you in this region. Ah, one day I will take you to the Mission House; have orders from the superior. Well, now we are coming on to this stony ground ; never noticed the round cactus before ; always grows here so. Greenhouse plant in some parts ; not so here. Well, well."

" Mr. Kirwan, look at that snake ! What kind is it ?"

" Oh, that's a rattlesnake."* The reptile was basking in the sun surrounded by five or six little ones. As soon

---

* *Crotalus* (Rattlesnake). In zoology, a genus of the class *amphibia,* order *serpentes.* There are five species of this genus. The one found in America is the *Crotalus Horridus,* or Banded Rattlesnake—abdominal plates, 167 ; dorsal, 23—the most venomous of the serpent tribe ; growth, greatest extent, 6 feet, but those of this length are seldom seen now. This snake is eaten by swine with impunity. It preys on birds and smaller quadrupeds. The rattlesnake produces its young in June or July, generally about twelve in number. By September they grow from nine to twelve inches in length, There is little doubt that it receives its young into its mouth, and swallows them in time of danger. This theory has been much laughed at by people who have not had ocular demonstration of the fact. M. Beauvois, a naturalist born *in the last century,* asserted this fact, and declares that " happening to disturb a rattlesnake in a walk near Pine Log, he saw it immediately coil itself up and open its jaws, when instantly five small ones, that were lying by, rushed into its mouth. He retired, and in the course of a quarter of an hour saw her discharge them. He approached it a second time, when the young retired into its mouth with greater celerity than before, and the snake immediately moved off into the grass and disappeared." The rattle consists of hollow, hard, dry, and semi-transparent bones, nearly of the same size and figure, resembling in some measure the shape of the *human os sacrum for,* although only the last or terminal one seems to have a rigid epiphysis joined to it, yet has every one of them the like, so that the tip of every uppermost bone runs within two of the bones below it, by which contrivance they have not only a moveable coherence, but also make a more multiplied sound, each bone hitting against the other two at the same time. The *C. dryinas,* or wood rattlesnake, inhabits America. *C. durissimus,* or striped rattlesnake, inhabits America, and is generally found under the trunks of fallen trees. *C. milliarius* inhabits Carolina. *C. mutus* inhabits Surinam.

as she perceived them she gave the rattle, opened her mouth to its widest extent, and in an instant the whole brood descended. Withdrawing on to the soft grass near, Woodhouse watched the young ones come forth from their living tomb, to which the wheels passing over the stones quickly bade them retire again.

"That's something you wouldn't see in England."

"Yes, it is."

"Well, in Texas and Missouri you will make acquaintance with the chameleon, the hideous lizard, and the classical salamander, or horned frog."

"And the prairie dog?"

"No; that lives generally in the arid soil of the Mauvaises Terres, where it has villages of its own."

"Villages!"

"Yes, friend Englishman, villages."

"You don't know much about the Mauvaises Terres. Well, I guess it's a kind of plateau, where the Little Missouri, the Mankizita Watpa, the Terre-blanche, and the Niobrarah take their rise."

"Well, I want to know about the villages of the prairie dog?"

"Every site of these villages extends over an area of several square miles of smooth table land, on which the grass is short and thin."

"Do they make houses?"

"Houses! Well, they pile up the earth round their dwellings about two feet above the surface of the soil to protect themselves against inundations, which in the rainy seasons would engulph them and their hopes."

"Well, that is odd."

"You would think it more odd did you see them tear up the grass round their houses, and leave the flowers only."

"I say, you must be cramming me."

"Cramming you! I assure you solemnly I have found the certain flowers which surround their little abodes spared with much taste. Prairie dogs are gardeners ; they leave the *Hedeoma Hirta*, the *Solanum Triflorum, Lupinus Pusillus*, the *Erigeron Divaricatum, Dysodia Chrysanthemoides, Ellisia Myctagenea*, and the *Panicum Virgatum*."

"I would not have believed this had I read it."

"I assure you it is solemnly true, also that they are governed by a Republic."

"Oh, that's too good."

"Nevertheless true that the several millions of prairie dog townships, full of life and motion, are governed as Republics."

"I can't believe it. But has this prairie dog, this resemblance to a squirrel, no amicable relations with other animals ? "

"Yes, with the rattlesnake and a small kind of owl, usually found at the entrance of their lodges."

"Ha, ha, ha! Has this dog no enemies ? "

"Yes, two, the wolf and the fox."

In conversation such as this the drive over the prairies passed rapidly away, and they were now nearing the creek on the banks of which the ranche to which they were proceeding was situated. They entered the little farm yard in front of the house, tied up the horse, and even there the low moan of some one in agony might be heard.

"Come with me," the doctor said to his companion, "to hear something of the rancher's life."

Sad and desolate the house looked as they crossed its threshold. A woman dying alone, miles from any woman, with no woman friend to stand by her sick bed, to aid her in those little luxuries of nursing so dear to us Europeans, when coming from some loved hand.

Half caste—half Indian, half French, she lay dressed upon her un-made bed; her long, dusky tresses fell around a face of rich beauty, almost startling in its intense pitifulness, refined by pain. It seemed so sad, she so young, attended by her husband, a rough Irishman, who was too grief-stricken even to minister that material assistance he might have given.

The ashes were grey and cold in the American stove; the floor dirty and unswept; no bread made*; no food prepared; and the man sat by the side of the wife hopelessly. "Would medicine do her any good?" he asked. As the doctor said he could only alleviate her sufferings, not cure them, the tears rained down that husband's face. He, so much older than his wife, loved her dearly. They made the fire, and cooked the bread cakes, tidied

---

* N.B.—In Kansas, on account of the great heat, bread was made fresh for every meal.

the room, and the half-caste thanked them by the eloquent tears rolling out of those lustrous eyes, undimmed by illness. She took her medicine passively; resigned mayhaps to death. She, taken into the Christian Church, knew she would find warmth, light, companionship, happiness, beyond the bare walls of the shed she called home, outside of that living palpitating flesh which enveloped her spirit.

They left, with regret, those two lone beings in their Ranche. Two days later the Irish Rancher within a few feet of his home, turned the sods with his spade, and the half-caste was laid to her rest by the hands of her husband, so much older than herself.

Brown Kirwan seemed to think some strange romance had linked those two lives together.

"Did anybody know her father?"

"Yes, he was one of the traders in buffalo skins amongst the savages."

"Do they ever marry with the Indians?"

"Unfortunately, yes; young Englishman. I believe the law stands thus: If they marry an Indian wife they have a right to a claim of 150 acres, and a certain amount for every child born to them. Many marry a wife in every tribe they trade with, under different names. But this is in the lower class of traders, and I hope it will soon die out, as the civilisation advances and the Government more efficiently grapples with the difficulties of government on the extreme limits of her great States. What of the Indian

life can be civilized will be, as for example the Cherokees, who now make good farmers, &c., and are settled
on their claims. What cannot be civilized will be
extinguished by the rapid advance of civilisation, which
must in time extend to the shores of the Pacific."

They were driving now through the rich sunshine, the
air seemed heavy with the fragrance of the flowers, and
everything appeared so health-giving that the thought
of death, pain, and corruption was out of place in such
a time, and on such a day. Silence had fallen on them
awhile, when Brown Kirwan roused his friend's attention
by saying : "I dream sometimes of things in the future."

"Do you ; but you can't believe in that unreal world
of sleep ?"

"I dream, and my dreams come true, Woodhouse."

"And what particular dream haunts you now ?"

"Only this one—I saw you distinctly in my dreams
long before you came this way, I saw you sitting by my
dead body in a prairie ranche, snowed up. I saw you
take my coffin in an ox waggon over the prairies, and,
what is more, I believe a strange fatality has brought
you into this neighbourhood, and you must go through
all I have seen in my dreams. You could not resist
coming, you were drawn by a stronger sympathetic power
than your own—over land and sea—and I firmly believe
for this purpose."

Woodhouse laughed—"There is a purpose in everything God allows, Mr. Kirwan, and that I am prepared
to grant. I am afraid, though, that dispiriting ranche

scene has affected your spirits—something unusual for a Doctor that. But I must tell you a dream tale I heard from an English farmer : A person saw his dead father in his sleep, he went to consult a doctor, the doctor naturally asked what his patient had had for supper the previous evening ? Half a pork pie, was the answer. Ah, replied the doctor—ah, well, my dear sir, go and eat the other half to-night, and you will see your poor dear dead mother.

Brown Kirwan smiled, and with terrible earnestness replied : "Ah yes ; I dare say, cause and effect. My dream was too distinct, though, and it will come true."

> "Sunt geminæ somni portæ: quarum altera fertur
> Cornea, quâ veris facilis datur exitus Umbris:
> Altera, candenti perfecta nitens elephanto;
> Sed falsa ad cœlum mittunt insomnia Manes."
> *Æneidos*, Lib. VI., l. 893.

CHAPTER III.

"What have we toiled for? Fame—
"The echo of a name,
"To be forgot with easy unconcern
"When the quick flame, whose ray
"Illumes our thinking clay,
"Fades, and we shrink into the quiet urn,
"No more on this poor stage to smile or sigh,
"At woman's flattering voice, or man's ascetic eye."
J. H. Wiffen, "Inquisition of the year."

A GLIMPSE ONLY.

LIFE in the Ranche proceeded in the same quiet way as usual—and Willie Woodhouse had in a few weeks grown into the life, which at first struck him as being so repugnant. Before sun-rise the fire was alight in the American stove, bread being prepared for breakfast, luscious coffee berries roasted, and the coffee made. Pork would be fried, corn bread made, and men with hearty appetites—master, guest, and servants—sat down at the same table. What merry and happy breakfasts they were, can be imagined. A stray newspaper now and again would find its way into the company, and all questions under dispute were referred to Charley, who was the President of this little Republic. Sometimes the breakfast would be later, for the men had orders to go and feed the cattle first, Charley Kirwan being a cattle rancher. As he said he placed a horse for riding at the disposal of his guest, who, with books, exploring the country round, long walks and conversations with his host, found those first days full of excitement and all too short. Kirwan was a man of the world whose experience was both large and varied. Born not far from the triple cities of New York, Brooklyn and Jersey; at an age when most boys are still at school, he had started in life on his own account, and refused all help, but his own, to forward himself in life.

Whatever he took in hand seemed to prosper. Finally he entered into partnership with a lawyer in Chicago, and finding he had made money enough went West, and bought several claims for cattle farming (each claim contains 150 acres). Buying four bulls from Kentucky's famous herds, and some hundred of Texas cows, he started a strain of cattle famed in that western district. Charley, travelling in Europe, had left the care of his farms and cattle until recently to his younger brother, Henry, who a few months before this story opened had succumbed to that deleterious enemy prairie fever, or ague, caught mostly from turning the virgin soil whilst following the plough. The soil being so rich, emits gases which poison the system. At least this is the prairie theory. Quinine is the great antidote.

Kirwan was a man whose thoughts ran far below the surface of ordinary humanity, a man who appreciated true æsthetics, but who cordially despised sentimental æstheticism. From the study of law, his thoughts had turned to other studies; amongst these studies being the then vexed question of Catholicism. He ultimately embraced that faith, and settled down near the Roman Catholic Mission amongst the Osages, just within the then frontier. Whilst in Europe he had invited his friend to join him for some few months.

On this particular morning in question Kirwan proposed duck shooting on the creek at some short distance from the back of the house. Whilst the two friends were wandering quietly in the canes and bushes there, and Kirwan succeeded right and left in bringing down his game, Lieboldt came to say:

"A shentleman wants yer, Sharley."

"Who is he?"

"I don't know, he cum afther them carfves."

It was a Canadian farmer and his son who came to enquire about buying eighty calves.

"Yes, I can oblige you, my friends," replied Kirwan, "they are not here, but at the upper ranche," and then turning to his friend he invited him to come and see some calf-separating. "It's hard riding, friend, and a vicious cow might horn you."

"I'll take my chance with the rest of you."

"Well, then, we number six, and the two men at the other ranche count eight. Yes, we can do it."

"Come in and have coffee, corn bread, and pork, then we can start for the upper ranche."

Uproariously they chatted whilst the meal was in preparation under their eyes, and then doing full justice to it, the cavalcade started for a few miles ride, mostly over the edge of the great prairie, here and there dotted with a tiny ranche. By degrees the ranches became fewer, the cultivation less, and then the broad expanse in all its vastness burst upon their eyes. Rich luxuriant vegetation indeed; over this vast stretch Kirwan's cattle ranged for miles, watched by the ranche boys, and at night were driven home to their carels.*

This upper ranche was built in a more picturesque manner than the lower one. It had a wooden portico and garden behind, though only one ·room. Great white-hearted cabbages grew here in the garden, which they ate raw with salt, and which also served for making into sour kraut. The stables and outhouses were nearer the ranche than in the lower one, and the carel built close by, so that if cattle stealers came near in the night, the dogs' barking could easily be heard by the men in charge. It was late when they arrived, and the strangers went directly off to see the herd; beautifully fat and sleek they looked, feeding in their large groups, as they were driven gently home for the night.

The bargain was struck there, and the calf separation from the cows was to begin early in the morning.

---

* Carel, an enclosure in which cattle are penned for the night.

The long ride had made all hungry, and how to cook any supper was a difficulty ; no matches could be found for some time on the shelves in the ranche, and when found they showed plainly no meat, and it was late in the evening already.

To the dark hen-house some of the party went, and in twenty minutes two fowls skinned and ready for the pot lay upon the table. One engaged in bringing wood in, one engaged in fetching water in, one making bread, one coaxing up the fires, one washing up the breakfast things, how quickly the time sped. Then a savoury odour floated to hungry nostrils, and there was laughter, a merry supper, tobacco fumes and coffee fragrance mingling.

Then night, silence, and deep slumber.

At early dawn the astonished Texan mother cows beheld their carel invaded by twelve horsemen, and then the mad chase of separation began. Now it was the red calf to be hunted from its mother and the line kept, now the black and white, or red and white calf, until the perspiration streamed from the reckless riders, and the lather showed plainly on the sides of Texan horses.

"Do you enjoy it, Englishman ?" asked Kirwan, as exhausted he paused to wipe his forehead, and rest his Texan cob.

"Yes, thanks, friend Kirwan, muchly."

"Well, it's a glimpse only we are giving you of our life. More enjoyable than studying for fame in your old world, eh ? this healthful exercise. How often have I in the museums and churches of the old world, or the indolent life of hotels and sight-seeing, longed for such exercise as this. It puts new life into one—new energy."

"Well, certainly it makes one eat and sleep well."

"Yes, and forget fame, and the heart-ache fame brings, and I think, at least my experience is, it makes one love God better—at least it does me—me, Charley Kirwan."

CHAPTER IV.

"When reapers unto reapers calling
Tell the rich harvest of the grain they bring,
Shall we forget how snow and sleet were falling
On those tired toilers of the bitter spring.

He murmured not! in earthly races
To winners only do the heralds call;
But oh! in yonder high and holy places
Success is nothing, and the work is all.

Here be unrecorded
The work he fashioned, and the path he trod;
Here, but in heaven each kind heart is rewarded,
Each true name written in the Book of God!"—*F. W. F.*

THE MISSION HOUSE.

IN a picturesque grass-grown cemetery on the banks of the Neosho, sloping so gently from the steep river bank towards the little town of Osage, the westering sun throws tree shadows over an un-named grave. No tomb-stone marks it; tall grasses wave over it, and shelter sweet-scented wild flowers; and yet it is a grave to which the heart of many an Indian turns, over which many a settler has shed a tear.

I mean the grave of J. J. Bax, of the Society of Jesus, the earthly corner-stone upon whom this Mission is built.

Brave warrior of God; athlete of an everlasting gospel. I have only known thee from thy reflexion in the souls of uncouth men; and so powerful was the Grace of God in thee, that I a stranger to thee write thy name with reverence and love.

This dead man, lying in his grave, shall tell the story of his dear Osages. I take briefly extracts from letters of his written between June, 1850, to 1852:

"Father Schoenmackers, myself and three coadjutor brothers, quitted S. Louis on the 7th of April, 1849, and arrived safely on the banks of tho Ncosho, a tributary of the Arkansas, situated about 130 miles from Westport, frontier town of the state of Missouri.

"The trial was very severe to us who were entering for the first time into the immense prairies of the Indians, which we had only measured according to the deceptive images of our imagination. The reality appeared different. We endured hunger, thirst, and cold. For a fortnight we were obliged to pass our nights in the open air, in the dampest season of the year, each having naught for a bed but a buffalo hide and a single blanket. On the 28th of April we reached our destination, to the great delight and surprise of the Indians. At the first sight of these savages, and finding myself surrounded by these children of the desert, I could not suppress the pain I felt. I saw their sad condition."

"On our arrival we found the houses unfinished, very inconvenient, and much too small for a great number of the children; they were also very badly situated, not

being in the centre of all the villages which compose
the Mission. The population of the tribes comprised
under the name of Great Osages and Little Osages is
nearly 5,000 souls, of whom 3,500 reside on the banks
of the Neosho, and the others on the Verdigris, a smaller
river than the Neosho, although the valleys and prairies
it waters are more favourable to culture."

"Immediately after our arrival our first care was to prepare a school. It was opened on the 10th of May. The
first who came to our school being very happy, many
others followed; and before the close of the year in a
house built for twenty persons only, we were obliged to
lodge fifty children. The nation then assembled, and
requested the agent to petition their Great Father to
enlarge the houses of the Mission. The Government ac-
ceded to this demand."

In 1852 an epidemic swept through the nation. Of
nearly 1500 savages who fell victims to it almost all received the sacraments of the Church. Seized at last himself with the same illness, Bax continued his ordinary
labours and dragged himself around to visit the sick and
dying. He was dying and still laboring. During five
years he instructed and baptized more than 2000 Indians.
He instructed neophytes with great care and pains-taking
assiduity. His charity so gained all hearts that the
savages call him only by the beautiful word which in
Osage means, "the Father who is all heart."

Thus far for the foundation of my story.

That same westering sun glinting through the leaves

in that far cemetery, goldening the grass over the graves of Indians and settlers alike, falling lovingly on the rough railed-in addition where lie the priests and brothers, who after tired labors have entered into the stillness of that rest which remaineth for those who have loved much, and served the Great King truly, the light from that same sun fell on the rough buildings of the Mission : irregular constructions, of no architectural pretentions, yet with their angularities softened by this light, and forming no unpleasant picture. There was the long, low church, with its dark walnut-wood fittings, and three blocks of houses.

In the middle block, in a tiny room, sat the aged Superior of the Mission. His features were irregular, yet that life of strange self-denial lent to them that calm expression one sees on faces when self has been utterly conquered. An expression more fascinating than that skin-deep beauty of a few years, for this expression deepens in attraction as the furrows of age claim kinship with it. He was dressed in an ordinary black suit, and was smoking his pipe. In this tiny room the furniture consisted of a bed, two chairs, a rough stove, a writing table, a bookcase, and some strange construction that did duty for a ward-robe.

Death follows quickly on the trail of civilisation to the Indians. Fire-water (whisky) has laid low its army of victims, and round the Mission proper, decimated of its original population by epidemic, has grown up a little town of settlers of many nationalities—Irish predominating. Brown Kirwan had settled in this colony as a surgeon and physician.

Well known was he for his kindly disposition, and well liked too by the old Superior of the Mission, who reigned king-like in this Mission, as was Kirwan president-like at the Ranche.

A knock came to awaken the Superior out of his thoughts—a knock at his door.

"Come in." And Brown Kirwan entered.

"Take a seat, my friend, and have a pipe too."

"Don't smoke at this time."

"Well, I'm pleased to see you; how goes the long parish? Room for your evolutions in this great tract of country; large parish this, some hundred miles square."

"Yes, you must have had enough of riding in your time."

"Aye, and work for you, too." Then he took his pipe from his mouth, looked at it thoughtfully, and twisted his tongue round the stumps of teeth age had left to him; a common habit of his this.

"Aye, and work for you, too; work for you, too, although you saw a lot in war."

"What kind—eh, sir?"

"Cholera along the river Kansas, at West Port, and in places round."

"But how did that affect the Osages?"

"They were panic-stricken, and sought safety in the plains."

"And the children?"

“Were left here under the care of us Blackgowns.”

“Strange !”

“Yes, they came, saying : ‘Blackgown, take our children, they will be safe under your care, and protected by the son of God and His Mother.’”

“I wonder they didn’t apply the same theory to themselves.”

“I would they had done so. The cholera declared itself in a most terrible manner in their new abode, and carried off numbers.”

“Poor things.”

“Yes” (and tears rose in the old man’s eyes), “they hastened to return to us, but in such precipitation that they made no provision, and travelled day and night— day and night” (and a tear stole down his face), he continued, “in proportion as they reached their own lands, the scourge diminished. The last death was fifteen miles from the Mission, but I should have had work for you, taking you with me to meet them. Ah me—Ah me.”

“I heard you had measles here, too.”

“Ah well, yes. Forty-five in the boarding school fell sick in three days and a half—that was nothing much. But then the measles disappeared and were followed by putrid fever. That was in ’52.”

“Did many die ?”

“On Passion Sunday, the saddest of my life, we had two corpses laid out, and twelve children in danger of death. Eleven fell victims in a short time, and then the contagion spread amongst the Indians—the mortality was great indeed. Ah, Doctor, we had need of you then, and now we have passed that fearful crisis, you could hardly fire off a pistol anywhere round without hitting some man who professes to be a doctor."

"Well, certainly there are many here."

"Many indeed ; they follow the settlers."

"Were you repaid then for your troubles amongst the Indians ?"

"Yes ; I never witnessed such fervour on death beds as exhibited by our neophytes—they were models. I firmly hope and believe they already enjoy the presence of God, and I, shortly going that long journey, pray to see them again. But enough of all this. How is your brother's guest ?"

"Well and happy for a European in that rough Ranche life ; I introduced him to some sick there one day."

"Bring him to see me ; I want to know him ; bring him in to dinner, or to sleep."

"Thank you, I will do so ; I shall be up there with my Buggy shortly, and will drive him down."

"The supper bell is ringing—you will sup with us to-night ?   Come along, man, let us go."

Reader, let us, too, follow them.

It is a long, low room, white-washed, and dimly lit, chilly too ; yet standing on each side of a long deal table awaiting the Superior we can see three priests, and several lay brothers. Only forms are there for sitting upon ; chairs are at a premium.

The old man enters, points silently to the place his

visitor is to occupy, and then his kindly voice mumbles forth the Grace.

A lay brother reads a few verses from Holy Scripture, and commences a chapter from Rodriguez " On Christian Perfection."

The Superior taps upon the table with the handle of his knife, the reading ceases, and in honour of the visitor he announces " Talking" at supper instead of Reading.

A strange gathering that, drawing together under one roof men of such opposite dispositions, nationalities, and characters—men who could only live thus; cemented together by rule, yet apart from each other, as brick is mortared apart from brick by the Divine Meditation upon the Holy Gospels; layers of charity were between them; layers of undimmed truth cemented them together as one whole body, represented by the name of " The Society."

Take from them, burn, do away into chaotic night of forgetfulness that Gospel, and ye will perceive how rude anarchy would reign here.

See that Italian successful missioner of savages: what holds he in common with yonder Irishman, who knows so well how to deal with settlers only. See that curl of irony upon the lips of the great traveller of the Prairies, that American-Irish Priest opposite. What has he in common with the others? And the pioneer Superior—What does his Belgian intellect, sharp as a needle even now, hold in common apart from religion with his community?

Has that Italian, skilled in the fine arts of Italy, learned in science and a man of the world, aught in common with those lay brothers so cumbersomely feeding themselves yonder?

Yes! the love, example, life, death of a Man · who was a malefactor according to law, a Man who though dead eighteen hundred years, and done to death shamefully, has left tracks of light upon the lonesome pathway of this world: so much so that eighteen centuries have not sufficed to efface His life, death, and miracles. And where the blood pulsates red and ruddy through human hearts, there is His love felt.

Brown Kirwan felt this: as he sat at that rough table, listened to the conversation of men so strangely dissimilar to those who had thus far crossed his pathway in life, he could not help admiring that nobility of character which had thus far out in the Prairies drawn them into a community to do good to their fellow men.

It was strange to hear of Savages who would come two or three hundred miles to bring a child to Baptism: of one squaw in particular who swam creeks and walked hundreds of miles to have her baby baptized.

It was strange to hear of confessions—he who did not believe in confession at all; and yet even savages did? and were they taught right, or was he?

"And how, Padré Pinsotti, do they remember their sins?"

"They tie a piece of string round their waist, and in this cincture at intervals are little bundles of wood, like our matches; each bundle represents a certain sin, and as they sin so they add one more spike of wood to the bundle that sin represents. And as they proceed in their confession they say, 'Father, that is such a sin, count the bundle and you will know how many times I committed it.'"

Brown Kirwan laughed a hearty laugh. It was something so novel to him; and the company, descrying the impression this recital had made, told him strange stories of the Prairie life, and invited him on the morrow to see their pig shooting and salting fray: from twenty to forty fat pigs to be laid in salt for the house and school during the next year.

"Who shoots them?"

"Why one of our scholars."

"An Indian?"

"No, one of our settlers' sons."

And now the Irish Priest tells how many hundred dollars he has gathered together in collections during his last absence — collections made amongst the poor Irish engaged on the great Prairie Railroad to the Far West.

And then Quinlin was chaffed as being the best gatherer of worldly pelf among the poor.

And thus ends a pleasant supper, and Brown Kirwan takes new thoughts away with him, out of the low white-washed Refectory of the Jesuits.

CHAPTER V.

"Behold of what delusive worth,
  The bubbles we pursue on earth,
  The shapes we chase
  Amid a world of treachery!
  They vanish ere death shuts the eye,
  And leave no trace."
          "*Coplas de Manrique.*"—*Longfellow.*

THE STORED GOLD — WHAT CAME OF IT.

TOM was sweeping the floor of the lower Ranche. Tom in rough knee boots, knee breeches, and his cloth shirt, and Tom was only doing this during the interval, whilst the bread that he had made was cooking in the small stove. Tom in his vigorous way of sweeping sent out great clouds of dust which almost obscured the bright sunshine, creeping in through the open door and window. Tom laughed: "Who'd her believed I'd her done this six weeks ago. He's a rum 'un though, he don't mind work, he don't, he-he-he. He can saddle his horse now, and bake bread, and make bread, and sweep the floor, and we's a taught him all that. Well, he do know summat—he and Charley do.

There you dust get hout. Wants me to learn my caterchisum do he ! ! ! Asked how many persons there are in God—persons or pussons? Pusson, well I'se a pusson. How many pussons in God? Seven I says— seven pussons. He looked grave too when I sed it ; then I looks at the caterchisums and finds its only three. Who'd a thort it. It were seven sacraments I meant. He weren't cross though."

"Tom, fetch some water from the creek."

It was Charley Kirwan's voice disturbing Tom's theological reverie. Charley was dressing after a long ride from his upper ranche. Woodhouse had gone with a book for a long read on the bank of the creek, and to watch the mud tortoises sunning themselves on the fallen trees lying in the water.

Winter had not yet crept over the Prairies, the Indian summer was lengthening itself out strangely this year, and Charley Kirwan, wise man, knew that a very severe winter would follow on the trail of this long delicious Indian summer. With forethought had he stacked his corn cobs near where the winter feeding would be ; the hay was all that could be desired for the long winter, both in quality and quantity. He had sold off most of his calves, and engaged a new man, Hecker, who was coming in in a few days. Everything spoke fairly of prosperity. His money was out at a good interest with the settlers round, and now this coming winter he would enjoy himself in hunting, skating, and all healthful prairie sport—"mais l'homme propose, Dieu dispose."

Charley was exuberant ; glad, too, his friend was enjoying himself on the prairies.　What could he do to amuse him to-day ?　Ah, yes ; he would take him to Button's and have a meal there.

"Tom,—Tom ! "

"Yes, Charley."

"Is that bread baked, and the prairie chicken cooked ?"

"Yes, and I've got beans too, and fresh water in, and the things washed."

"All right, Tom, you're not a bad fellow."

Tom scratched his head.　"Charley, is it seven pussons in God and three sacraments, or three pussons in God and seven sacraments ?"

"What made you think of that ?"

"Why that ere friend of yourn is a teaching of me religion.　I dunno much of it.　When I'm stupid he don't kinder say much, but looks at me in such a sad way, that makes me wanter learn more.　He sez to me t'other day : 'Tom, are yer baptized ?'　I sed, 'What's that ?'　Then he splains it, and I remember in Ohio, afore I come this way, the clergyman did come, mother sez, and made me a member of the Church.　But how, mother never told me, and now she's dead, and I'm an orphan, I want to know more."

"I'se shay Sharley, mine mule lost.　Have you seen hur," and the imperturbable face of Lieboldt appeared at the window.

"You goes to eat, Sharley."

"Your mule's all right ; I rode her this morning, and now she's feeding in the stable by the Creek."

" All right, Sharley. You have the schicken for eat,
I think I like some too."

" Go find my friend, and then come back with him
to dinner."

This Lieboldt did quickly, as all interest to him at
that moment centred around the " schicken." Poor
schicken, nought was left of him shortly but bones,
which Lieboldt sucked eagerly, remarking—" Hur has
done mine body goot."

" Now bring me the ox waggon quickly, Tom, I
want to get away; and you and Lieboldt can go about
the fencing I told you of this morning."

Shortly an ox waggon drew up at the door—none
of your English waggons, but a strong Prairie article,
rude in construction, useful in occupation. Charley and
Woodhouse mounted, and started off in the direction
of the wooded Creek. You carriage-driving community
little know the intense enjoyment of such a ride, in
spite of joltings experienced on unmade roads and
crossings of bridgeless streams. On such a day as this
the air seemed sick with very sweetness, yet not nau-
seous, but exuberant withal and exhilarating. Out from
the heat in amongst the richly-wooded stretch by the
creek, with embroidered shadow patterns from the trees
falling over them, how healthful and happy those two
men looked : then at the crossing, the water bubbled
and murmured over stones, and the sound was music
to them.

This was truly one of those deep, cool enjoyments

of life into which one sometimes sinks, with which some of our hours are gilded in this shadow life of earth. Life seems to stay still and lave herself in an enjoyment too deep for speech, to brace herself up for some deep coming trouble.

How often have you, my readers, noticed this in life? How often has this been your own fate? the calm before the fierce violence of the storm bursts full upon you.

Presently Woodhouse's voice broke up Charley's deep silence:

" Charley, whose ranche was that we passed lying so cool and well kept in amongst the fruit trees? It looks so different to yours. There is an air of that European refinement you don't believe in about it."

" Whose ranche is it? The ranche of a man who plays a dangerous game in these parts. He stores gold. He thinks he had best be his own banker. He has no faith in humanity."

" Why dangerous?"

" Because we have only ourselves to carry out law here : no organised police force, and we ourselves collectively in this frontier life represent law and justice. For certain crimes we lynch ; over other things men call crimes we draw a broad curtain, because in this new prairie life, composed of so many discordant elements, we cannot drag together the practical European law courts. As our society developes, so will the principles which cement society."

"True; then I agree with you the aforesaid Rancher plays a dangerous game. Does he mix much with others?"

"No; he means storing gold, and then going to live in New York State."

"You all seem to like him?"

"Yes, he has a keen intellect, arithmetically keen, as those straight lines of trees planted about his Ranche show you."

"You see somewhat of Cube Root there, Charley?"

"And Addition too."

"Charley! Charley!"

"And Multiplication each autumn."

"*You are* incorrigible."

"Yes, but between each row you see Division."

"Please don't."

"Yes, and in autumn Great Common Measure, and sometimes Profit and Loss."

"Please don't talk so; but tell me, if you won't talk about this man, something of these Buttons we are going to see."

"Ah, yes. Well, Button—middle-aged man, formerly a stone cutter or carver in Ohio, made some money, came West like the rest of us; antecedents unknown; wife short, homely, good house-wife; several daughters, good nice girls; two sons, good hard-working fellows, one has a claim of his own. But enough of that, you'll soon see them."

They now crossed the creek again at a sort of ford, evidently with an artificial bottom.

"Some of Button's work this?"

"Yes, sharp fellow Button, as you'll see:" and Charley pointed to a road one side of which was fenced in, and on the other side was a neat hedge. "Something like, that, eh?" And behind the hedge one could see a goodly store of fruit trees, and amongst the trees bee-hives, and beyond the bee-hives a long low thatched building—Button's Ranche—and, off the building, cow-sheds and cart-lodges. "Sharp fellow, Button, eh?" said Charley, again pointing to the Ranche.

Now a great dog howled, announcing their approach, and a woman's shrill voice called out to Kirwan: "Welcome, Charley; we are glad to see you and the stranger." Without more ado she shook hands, reaching up to them in the waggon. "Stranger, Tom (Charley's ranche boy) says your name is Willie, that's what I shall call you. How do you do, Willie? You come and eat my apples, pears and other fruit when you like. You're welcome to a meal when you can come." And thus she talked on until Charley, her favorite, said—"Where's the old man?" "Oh, he's a choppin a wood not far off." "And the boys?" "Oh, they'll be home from plough directly. Come in, and I'll make some tea bread such as Charley likes whilst I talk to you. The girls are busy inside, sewing. So now you know all."

The oxen were foddered; and in the large square kitchen the family were after awhile grouped around the table, eating delicious buck-wheat cakes, bacon, jam, dried apples and peaches, and what not else hospitable Mrs. Button had gathered out of her stores, which seemed illimitable. And such coffee she poured out! thinking more of her guests' comfort than of the common garb she wore; and the girls were like her—"good nice girls," as Charley said—whose ages ranged from twenty-one to seventeen. Ted Button large-framed and handsome, about twenty-two. Tom dark-skinned, handsomer than his brother, about eighteen, with a nature bubbling over with fun.

The conversation turned upon all prairie subjects, and laughter rippled in waves around the merry board; until Charley, looking at Button, said—"My friend wants to know who lives in the Ranche near the Creek, with the straight lines of trees about it."

Then silence fell on them all, and a palpable shiver went the round of the table, until Button Senior spoke out—"Did you tell him?"

"I did not tell him all. I spoke in the present. I said a man lived there who stored up gold. If I told him, I might frighten him away from us."

"Best to tell him," said bluff Button, "he will only hear from some less authentic source."

Mrs. Button, too, leant over and said—"Yes, tell him what came of it, what came of the stored-up gold!"

"Well, Mrs. Button, what came of it?"

She leant forward and whispered in his ear: "Murder on Murder!"

He smiled an incredulous smile back at her. "All

right, Mrs. Button, you don't frighten us Europeans thus."

She laughed at his incredulity, whilst the party enjoyed it. Charley looked over at him from his side of the table and said—"Don't ask another word until I speak of it to-morrow."

"You *will* tell me ?"

In clearly firm-cut words he answered, "*I will.*"

And on the morrow he did.

CHAPTER VI.

"Placidaque ibi demum morte quievit."—*Virg.*

There calm at length he breathed his soul away.

WHAT CHARLEY KIRWAN TOLD HIM.

THE breakfast table in Kirwan's ranche deserted. Kirwan is smoking his pipe, sitting close to the wood fire ; snowy, flakey wood ashes lie at his feet on the hearth stone, which never knew the luxury of a fender ; quiet crimson tongues of flame crept in and out of the crevices left by logs piled there in careless profusion.

Woodhouse sat by the window reading the Æneïd of Virgil, with English notes, critical and explanatory, by Anthon, edited by Trollope.

This was one of the quiet hours in which they seldom spoke to each other. Kirwan took his pipe from his mouth, surveyed it carefully, watched the rings of smoke creeping up to the ceiling, and then said:

"Willie !"

4

The eyes of his guest turned to him with astonishment written in them—that Kirwan should thus break through that still hour by talking.

"You're surprised, but you wished to hear of Acton's Ranche."

"Acton's ranche?"

"Yes, the one we passed yesterday."

"Oh, ah, yes, do tell me," said he, hastily laying down his book, "that one Mrs. Button was so mysterious yesterday evening about; quite novelesque, eh! man with a lot of money. 'Murder on Murder,' &c., &c."

"Well, old fellow, she was quite right. Only a few weeks ago, there actually was a murder committed there."

"By the Indians?"

"No."

"How then; did Acton make away with himself, or what?"

"He did neither. He was made away with, or rather his life was."

Kirwan noticed the slight shudder that crept through the body of his guest, and wondered whether he had done wisely to speak of this without a greater preparation. He had left his seat by the window, and was sitting on a low stool facing him.

"Will you tell me all about it, Charley?"

"Yes; I will. Acton came into this district some few years ago, one of the first settlers; he built his house more on the European cottage model, with every comfort he could then place in it. You know the roughness of our prairie life by this time. Well, he planted a garden about his house, the one you so admired, and then he set to work on his claim. Everything he did seemed to prosper, and he made considerably of gold by fruit and the cultivation of his land. The neighbours were all partial to Acton; he was ready to give others a helping hand, or place the secrets of his success at their disposition. A fellow he was, good all the way round; just such a man who should thrive in a prairie home. Most settlers near grew to know him, and to like him. Still, he had no faith in anything in the Mission in the way of banks to store his money, and foolishly he kept it in his Ranche. That was all well and good, so long as he was sure of the laborer, or help he had about him. I suppose his help must have left, as others do when they have gained somewhat of money, and gone in search of a claim of his own farther up country. At all events, a time came when Acton was left without help. He did as well as he could for awhile, assisted by the neighbours; but shortly their own work called them away, and for love or money he could get no one.

"One evening entering his Ranche tired out, and chopping wood upon his door-step, by the dying light, to coax up a fire, with which to cook his supper by, he was accosted by a neighbour who had heard of a young fellow in want of work, a stranger to them all, going down West. Did he care to engage him? if so, the neighbour would see that he called in in the morning.

' Why in the morning, friend,' said Acton, ' bring him round to-night, and then in the morning he can, if he suits me, set about his work.'

" Well, as you like. We know nothing of him—he is a stranger to us—simply travelling down West— comes and asks a meal of victuals, and my old woman immediately says, ' Maybe he'd do for neighbour Acton.' He's strong, burly, and a stranger : that's all we know. It may be dangerous taking in a stranger, where he has all to gain and nothing to lose. Beggars though, can't be choosers, and my work is standing still for want of hands, and my fruit and vegetables rotting. Well, neighbour Acton, think of it to-night, and to-morrow I'll see that he comes round."

" Acton did think of it, over his solitary tea in his ranche, and decided to give the stranger a trial, going to bed looking eagerly forward to the morrow.

" Early the next morning the stranger came : a man strong and burly, all that Acton wanted, but was he honest ? This thought flashed through his mind as he hired him straight off. That could only be proved by acquaintance with him.

" And so they set to work. Week after week passed by, and the stranger studied the life of Acton, until none of its secrets were hidden from him. His master grew to trust him, and he found out even where the money was kept. ' The love of money is the root of all evil.'· How, when, or where the idea first entered the stranger's head of obtaining possession of that money, no one ever knew. Certain it is, he must have brooded over it long.

"One day Acton, occupied in chopping wood with his hired man, was attacked from behind, and nigh killed with the blow of an axe ; indeed, so mangled that death ensued some short time after, and the man disappeared, taking the money with him. A neighbour passing some time afterwards goes to the Ranche door, and discovers the mutilated man, then in his death-agony—administers what comfort he could, and hears the dying man speak of that hope sure and fast, laid up in the great home of God, the Father's Ranche, where neither moth nor rust corrupteth more, and where thieves are powerless to break in, murder or steal ; and then all calmly he breathed forth his soul to God.

"The murderer had escaped, but justice must be done ; and so, mounting a horse, the man who had discovered the murder galloped from Ranche to Ranche, and spread the news far and wide. The Rancher left his ploughing, and every settler able to do so his occupation. To horse ! To horse ! They must hunt down him who so wickedly in cold blood had done that grievous murder ! Lumbering Dutch rifles, revolvers, guns of all ages and makes, were quickly loaded, and the self-organized army of justice swiftly grew and grew, until they reached at a fixed hour the Ranche where they should agree upon some settled way of scouring the country and arresting the murderer. Day and night should that search continue until he was lynched."

"I shot he, Sharley." It was Lieboldt, who had entered unperceived, and had heard somewhat of the conversation : for both the teller of the history and he who listened were far too much interested to have heard Lieboldt's entry.

"I shot he, Sharley, wid my old rifle. I were in the, hunt, I were." And Lieboldt continued the story: "We searched all the crick, the corn patches and buildings, whilst some galloped about in the prairie to see if he were in the long grass there lying hid. All that day we searched, but we didn't find he. We had watchers about all night, and in the early morning began agin. There in a woody bend of the crick we found he, and hunted he to a corn-stack. Shot after shot was fired—he and us stormed agin and agin. I felt the Dutch blood burn in my veins. 'We must have he if only we wait long enough.' And so we did. Young Garth fired and wounded he—then I fire, wounded he agin ; and so after desperate fight we take he. Not dead. Then we hold council whether we lynch he. 'Lynch he ! No,' cry some one, 'let's take him to the Ranche of Acton, and tie him in bed with the dead man, and let him die so. A warning to murderers that !' And so we did, and set a patrol before the Ranche and round it to see that no one aid he. And so he died, Sharley."

Here Lieboldt took what he wanted from the house, and retired murmuring something to himself.

"Is all this true, Charley ?"

"Why yes, man ! But Lieboldt didn't shoot him, I think. The wounds were revolver wounds, and the bore of the old man's musket is different to that. He is somewhat chaffed about, ' I shot he !' ever since the little bullet was discovered so different to his Dutch bore. But the hallucination rests."

"What a terrible story !"

"True, but we are obliged to administer the sternest justice here, or crime would be too common amongst us. Such a lesson was given by that man's death and his tragic end which lynching could never have given. The strangeness of it will be remembered, and stop crime close around us for a generation or two, and by that time law will be administered as in other parts of the States."

And so ended the conversation on Acton's Ranche, and the quick rush of coming events precluded all the further allusions to that subject which Kirwan's guest wished to make.

CHAPTER VII.

"From the contagion of the world's slow stain
We are secure, and then can never mourn
A heart grown cold,—a head grown grey in vain."

DINNER AT THE MISSION HOUSE.

BROWN Kirwan had not forgotten his brother's guest; indeed he was a frequent visitor at the Ranche during the long days of the Indian summer, and a great friendship had sprüng up between himself and Willie Woodhouse.

A week or so after the long ride and chat upon the prairies, he drove up to the Ranche, and invited Woodhouse to inspect the Mission House with him, as the Superior had specially invited him to dinner that day.

"An invitation from an unknown person, eh, Brown? Well, I must go. I will run down to the crick to see Charley; tell him I am going, and will be back shortly, and ready to go in ten minutes."

They drove in the early hazy morning back to the Mission. Much amused was the stranger with the Mission village. The plank footpaths, leading here, there, and everywhere ; the wooden houses of the settlers, the grim stone convent of the Lorettines standing facing the Square near which the foundations of the new church were already to be seen.

And as they drove into the Mission yard, there sunning himself in the beautiful sunlight stood the aged Superior of the Mission.

As Woodhouse stepped from the Buggy the aged man clasped both his hands in his. It seemed like Winter and Spring meeting, and out of reverence to him who had so long borne the burden and heat of the day the younger sank upon his knees, and the elder lifted his hands to heaven, placed them upon the bowed head, and blessed him. In that moment the souls of both of them seemed to have touched and known they were akin.

An unnatural piece of acting this might have been in others, but not so here.

All this had happened in less time than it takes to write, and hearty was the welcome given to the guests.

"You know nothing of our prairie life yet, Mr. Woodhouse ?"

"Hardly, Father ; yet enough to make me wish to know more."

"That's well. Has Charley taken you to the school at Walnut Creek ?"

"No. That I reserve for some winter evening."

"Ah, if the snow permits."

"But is the snow so very awful ?"

Brown and the Superior laughed.

"What think you of that telegraph wire buried?" asked the old man, pointing to the telegraph wires near them.

" Never !"

" Yes, indeed; and it drifts on the prairies to an enormous depth. We lose our prairie congregation then. Texan ponies are useless to bring them to us, or take us to them."

" I must take to my books."

" Or, as you are near the crick, to crick fishing."

" What, with the ice covering the creek ?"

" Yes. The creeks swarm with fish, and it is thus. The ice is, as a rule, clear as crystal ; and you see the fish ice-bound floating just beneath the ice, as they find no air-holes. With the broad back of an axe you strike the ice violently over where the fish's head is. This stuns him. You then cut away the ice in a square round the fish, large enough to insert a small sieve under its body. This, by practice, one learns to do so skilfully, that in an hour you may take as much fish as you can carry home with you."

A broad incredulous smile was on the face of Woodhouse. Brown Kirwan saw it, and assured him of the truth of this assertion and the enormous quantities of fish taken in this way by the Indians.

" Has he been to an husking party, Brown ?"

" No, not yet, Superior."

" Well, well, take him. The first one I saw many years ago amused me."

The sound of the bell called them now to the Refectory, where the Community joined them, coming in silently and falling into their allotted places.

The same long low room, white-washed, that Brown Kirwan knew before; only the sun-light streaming through the narrow windows, over the rough but appetizing fare, lent to the room warmth and cheerfulness.

The Blessing given, Quinlin the Priest read from Holy Scripture until he came to the verse, " Ye stand this day all of you before the Lord your God" (Paralip xxix., 10.)   Then the wonted signal for stopping the reading was given, and conversation began.

Brown started it by saying, " How quickly you are obeyed, Superior.   I notice as your signal is given the sound of the voice ceases—the word seems almost broken in two."

" Yes, that is the law of obedience : if we are writing and the bell rings for any duty, we leave off with the letter half formed."

Both the visitors looked surprised.

Quinlin said : " That is our rule ; we make it our duty to cheerfully accept obedience."

The Superior added : " The principle of the forest lies in the acorn, and the germ of every duty springs direct from the thought of God."

Pinsotti turned to Woodhouse, remarking : " From our early years God delegates some of His authority to our fellow men.   Primo to parents, and so on.   Respect for authority is a sacred duty, as well as a Divine command."

"Thermopylæ speaks of the obedience of the Spartans," said Woodhouse.

"Yes, the epitaph does:"

> "Go tell the Spartans, thou that passest by,
> That here obedient to their laws we lie."

"I have read," said Pinsotti, "the other day of true obedience. The armed skeleton of a poor Roman soldier was found in a recess near the gates of Pompeii. When the sulphurous storm broke over that guilty little city, how easy for him to have run away. But he wouldn't, because to escape would be to abandon his post without leave; and so that unknown hero just dropped the vizor of his helmet, and stood there to die rather than disobey."

"England is not behind-hand," said the doctor. "Don't I remember in our war, our men speaking of Balaclava," and glancing at his English friend he quoted:

> "Forward the Light Brigade,
> . . . . . .
> Theirs not to make reply,
> Theirs not to reason why,
> Theirs but to do and die—
> Into the valley of death
> Rode the Six Hundred."

"That proves obedience," said the Superior, "is not limited to the Church. We have these noble examples in the Army, of men preferring death to disobedience."

"And in the Navy also."

"Yes," said one brother, who had been awhile a sailor, "the wreck of the *Birkenhead*. A good ship crushed at sunset against a sunken rock; the boats few, and the water rushing in ; sharks thrusting horrid black fins through white breakers, the women and children shrieking, but the voice of the captain was heard calling the men to their ranks,—an order meaning death instantly obeyed. The boats left the vessel in order, taking the women and children to shore."

"I remember," observed Quinlin, "inch by inch the ship sank lower, the men stood calm, till one great wave rolled over her, and 'obedient unto death,' brave men, loyal indeed, sank to a noble burial."

"And if men in the world are obedient thus, what obedience should be observed by those in Holy Orders, and under the rule of a Society sanctioned by the Church ?"

"Aye, obedience, indeed," murmured the Irishman, and a sigh told his thoughts were about the subject of obedience, and what it cost him.

"Father Pinsotti, is it true about that discovery near Independence, in a Ranche there ? The Mission is ringing with the news this morning."

"Yes, too true, Mr. Kirwan. I myself have been in the Ranche ; in fact I tried to convert the people, and, indeed, it was I who gave them the prayer book found there, of which there has been much talk."

"What occupation were they ?"

"Well, nominally, they kept a grocer's store."

"And if any one came with money they let them down into that abominable trap ?"

"Yes, and in some way killed them there."

" And ?" asked a Brother, breathless.

" Buried them in their garden."

" How were they found out ?"

" Some one, after a heavy rain, saw marks as of graves settling down in their garden, and communicated with the police or military at Fort Scott, or some other place."

" And the military ?"

" Found it was only too true."

" I had the news through a European paper," said Woodhouse.

" And the law has dealt heavily with them ?"

" So heavily that such an enormity will never be perpetrated here again, we hope."

" Ah, my friends, five or seven graves, so many murders ; and I have been often to the house, but could make nothing of the people. The grace of God had never touched their hearts."

" And are you not afraid, Father Pinsotti ?"

" No, I have no fear. I can only die once ; and, endeavouring to honestly work in my Master's service, I know He will protect me."

In the meantime the dinner had duly progressed— the Irish stew, the roast meat, the stewed peaches, and cheese, were done full justice to, and now the signal given for silence, and the Martyrology read, they retired to the Church hard by, a long, low building, with its Sanctuary panelled in dark walnut wood, and there in silence all kneel before the Blessed Sacrament. Five minutes of silent prayer, and the Recreation began. This was the rule of the Osage Community.

A long and interesting conversation follows in the Superior's room, until the doctor suggests he must drive his friend home.

"Come again when you like," said the Superior, opening the door of the room next his own, a small cupboard-looking place containing a bed, a tub turned bottom upwards supporting a tin bowl and small ewer in tin. "This will be your room. Come and use it often; we shall be pleased to scc you. There is a stove in it too. You will be warm there, even in winter, Mr. Woodhouse."

"He will leave the Mission far behind him before then," exclaimed Quinlin.

"Hardly," said the Superior. "God has sent him to these parts for a purpose, and only when it is fulfilled will he leave."

CHAPTER VIII.

"The double night of ages, and of her—
Night's daughter—*Ignorance*, hath wrapt, and wrap
All round us."—*Childe Harold's Pilgrimage*.

    *   *   *   *

"He who ascends to mountain-tops shall find
The loftiest peaks most wrapt in clouds and snow;
He who surpasses or subdues mankind,
Must look down on the hate of those below.
Though high *above* the sun of glory glow,
And far *beneath* the earth and ocean spread,
Round him are icy rocks, and loudly blow
Contending tempests on his naked head,
And thus reward the toils which to those summits led."

   *   *   *   *   —*Byron*.

"In *His* great Name
I stand between thee and the shrine which hath
Had *His* acceptance.—" *Cain*."—*Byron*.

SUNDAY AND THE OSAGES.

A SUNDAY Morning at the Mission. Charley Kirwan and his guest are riding Texan cobs, and travelling at a smart pace to the Mission, to be in time for the service. As they near the vicinity of the Church they see people from the district going on the same errand. And what a laughable congregation of vehicles stand tenantless outside the Church! Such a group photographed would make a photographer's fortune in Europe.

Can feeble word-painting convey such grouping to the mind of a reader? Hardly. There stands the ox waggon and the oxen tethered to it ; the waggon itself looking like a miniature platform on wheels, and many like waggons in pretty groupings standing near in the large open space hard by the Mission buildings. Texan cobs too, saddled with Texan saddles ; and the makes and styles of Buggies various indeed. The neighing of the horses and the lowing of the oxen gave sound to the scene ; and these noises, intermingled with men's voices, came pleasantly to the ear ; whilst the deep blue tinted sky, the rich foliage not far distant, and the buildings of the Mission added the coloring necessary to make a very pretty picture indeed.

"Where do all these men come from, Charley?"

"From the country round—within a radius of from quarter of a mile to fifteen miles."

"One never sees them on a week day."

"No, they are Settlers and Ranchers. Whenever I come down here I find some one fresh, and that shows how quickly this district will fill up. The Indians will withdraw of themselves, and the Mission will be wholly left to the whites."

They did not tether their horses with the others, but rode on to Brown Kirwan's stable ; and having quickly dismounted and fed their horses, hastened to the Church.

What a sight! The long, low building, with its dark walnut-panelled Sanctuary, was crowded now

Swarthy Indians (Osages) were grouped in one part : tawny-skinned men with long, coarse, black hair floating nearly to the shoulders, and in their faces one read an awe-struck, solemn expression of wonder. As the sacred Office progressed at which they were assisting, the solemn look passed away, and in its place came one of love ; for boundless as the vast prairie is the love of the Indian to the Great Spirit. The rest of the building was filled in with settlers, predominantly Irish, with their wives and children. Here and there another nationality might be seen. But they were all bound together by the same religion, they were all permeated with the same devotion. On rude forms they sat, or else knelt on the bare floor ; but the conduct of the great congregation would shame most European churches.

Here was the life work of the old Superior. Here in this out-of-the-way place had he gathered into the Church savages who through the long night of ages had slowly groped their way to the stature of the knowledge of Jesus Christ. Here at last had they reached through the misty ignorance of heathenism, and felt the power of a strong sacramental life within them.

And those of other nations, here on the healthful prairie, away from civilization, had come to a truer and more practical knowledge of the Faith.

It was a holy and a wholesome thought indeed.

In the west end of the long low Church was the choir, composed of nuns and children from the Convent, who now and again, as the Office progressed, sang one of Faber's hymns to simple tunes that the people could follow.

Quinlin it was who preached an earnest sermon, and every word of it fell upon listening ears. How solemnly those words sounded in the otherwise still Church. "Forgetting those things which are behind;" and who amongst them had not something to forget, "reaching forth unto those things which are before." Ah, they were indeed all doing that; *some*, nay, *most*, reaching forth for gold which the rich prairie furrows should yield to them. "I press toward the prize to the high calling of God in Christ Jesus."

Were we all doing that? What a happy thought it was that none who enter that race are defeated; no rivalries enter into it; no jealousies how bitter soever spoil it; no failure embitters it. The prize was common to all, common as the sweet air that swept the wide prairie, and nobody would dispute their right to breathe that.

You have to win a race on which your life depends. Will you try to run it laden under a crushing burden? Will you try to do so with a log chained to your feet? No; you would free yourself from the obstacles. And so, in this life-long race we must all run, free yourselves from your sins—*your besetting sins.* How much easier you will run without these obstacles.

Thus did the sermon open that was listened to with greedy ears, and carried away to prairie homes, and into prairie lives.

The sermon ended, to the astonishment of those present, he said : " Before you are dismissed I wish to say a few words to you. A great epidemic is raging in the counties near us. In this wide country, where it is so difficult to obtain priests to administer to those about to die the Sacrament of Baptism at a moment's notice, know this according to the theology of the Catholic Church that, *in case of necessity*, where a priest cannot be had, any layman can baptize, be that lay person man, woman, or child. Only observe this. For the baptism to be valid, the water must be pure, *and you must say the words as you pour the water upon the head of the person you are about to baptize.* As you slowly pour the water, say the words instituted by Christ : ' I baptize thee in the name of the Father, and of the Son, and of the Holy Ghost.'

" And be careful in this, remembering Christ has said : ' Except ye be baptized of water, and the Holy Ghost, *ye cannot enter into the kingdom of Heaven.*'

" It is so necessary, that those dying without this Sacrament *cannot* enter into Christ's kingdom.*

" Be careful in this, and see that nobody departs hence unbaptized."

From the " Catechism of Christian Doctrine."
What is Baptism ?
Baptism is a sacrament by which we are made Christians, children of God, and members of the Church.
What other grace is given by this Sacrament ?
It cleanses us from original sin, and also from actual, if we be guilty of any.

Coming out from the Church the Superior invited Kirwan and Woodhouse to dinner, and afterwards to go to the Indian encampment on the banks of the Neosho. The Indians that day assisting at the Offices were a small contingent of Osages going to amalgamate with another Tribe.

At table the conversation turned on the Osages, and their capacities for acquiring knowledge. "Could they recite the Pater?"

"Some could, but Pinsotti had a way of teaching them. For the Creed he collected as many young Braves as there were clauses in it, and to each Brave he assigned one clause; twice a day, both at sunrise and sunset, they formed in line before the tribe and recited the symbol of the Catholic Faith. In the same way with the Pater and Ave. Thus the great truths of the Christian religion were daily before them."

"And is the Osage language difficult to learn?"

Can no one but a Priest baptize?

In case of necessity, when a Priest cannot be had any one may baptize.

How is Baptism given?

By pouring water on the head of the child whilst we pronounce the words ordained by Christ.

What are those words?

"I baptize thee in the name of the Father, and of the Son, and of the Holy Ghost."

What do we promise in Baptism?

To renounce the Devil, and all his works and pomps.

Is Baptism necessary for salvation?

Yes, for Christ says, "Unless a man be born again of water and the Holy Ghost, he cannot enter into the Kingdom of God" (John iii. 5.)

" You shall hear this afternoon."

" Are the Osages affable ?"

" Yes, it is natural to them to wish to live in peace and perfect friendship with everybody ; but they fight greatly with the Pawnee-Mahas. This is not a fault in the Osages, for the treatment they experience from the Pawnees would rouse even civilized nations."

" How so, sir ?"

" When the Osages go hunting, the Pawnees fall on the undefended villages, pillage the wigwams, and steal the horses. The Pawnees are very perfidious, and never keep to their treaties either."

" Yes," observed the Superior, " and the Osage carries his enmity against the Pawnee up to his death, for he always wishes, if not a Christian, to be buried on the highest slopes overlooking the enemies Hunting Grounds, so that even in death he may have the master-hood."

" Does not the nearness of the whites to the Savages have some effect for good ? "

" Unfortunately, no. Here as in Paraguay the contact with the whites makes the Indians more artful, plunges them deeper in vice, and because the Indian language has no blasphemous words in it, they actually curse God in a foreign language."

" How frightful ! "

" Yes, it makes it difficult for the Missionary," chimed in the Superior, " I remember Father Bax giving a Mission in a village named Woichaka-Ougrin (Cockle Bird). Whilst

he preached against Intemperance, and the evil conse-
quences of that habit, how it affected the health and was
the cause of sudden death, and displeased the Great Spirit,
Shape-shin-Kanouk (Little Beaver), the principal man of
the tribe, rose and said to him : 'Father, what you tell
us is true; we believe thy words; we have seen many
buried because they loved and drank fire-water (whiskey).
One thing astonishes us. *We* are ignorant ; *we* are not
acquainted with books ; *we* never before heard the words
of the Great Spirit; but the whites who have understanding, and know books, and who have always heard
the commandments of God, why do they drink fire-
water ? Why do they sell it to us ? Why do they bring
it to us when they know it displeases God and he sees
them ?'"

"Do you find them very troublesome to manage ?" asked
Kirwan.

"I think," replied the Superior (who dearly loved the
Indians), "if the Indians were treated with justice and
good faith they would cause little trouble. The Indians
complain of the dishonesty of the whites. The whites
banish them from their native soil, from the tombs of
their fathers, to which they are devotedly attached, they
take from them their hunting and fishing grounds. The
Indians must consequently seek what is wrested from
them, and build their wigwams elsewhere. They are
hardly at home in their new abode when they are removed
a second and third time. With each successive emigra-
tion they find their grounds restricted, and their fishing

and hunting places less abundant. The agents promise them protection and privileges never realized, and consequently .the savages call the whites 'forked-tongues,' or liars."

"Yes, it is hard lines on them indeed ; but I imagine as civilisation advances they will recede farther and farther until they touch upon the shores of the Pacific."

"Exactly so, according to the present system, but we shall never live to see things go so far as that. It seems to me, having studied them greatly in my character, as Superior of the Mission, that there is a feeble ray of hope for the preservation of a great number of them ; if the law proposed by Senator Johnson in 1854 is adopted in sincerity, both on the side of the Government and the Indians."

"What law was proposed ?"

"An establishment of three territorial governments in the Indian territory inhabited by the Choctaws, Creeks, Cherokees, the Chickasaws, and other tribes, with the provision of being admitted later on as distinct members of the confederated United States."

"What is the epidemic you spoke of, Mr. Quinlin ?"

"Pleuro-pneumonia and spino meningitis. It is not in the country yet, but surely it will come."

"Don't frighten us before it does come."

"No, no, no," said the Superior, and he touched the little bell near him to signify that "Talking" had finished.

After the short visit to the Church, they started for the Neosho to see the Indian encampment.

How pleasant it was walking through the fresh air, blowing up so pure and fragrant from the prairies, down by the banks of the Neosho, and into the thick pleasant foliage, where the temporary shelters stood, and then to see the Indians. The adults had only a slight covering over the middle of their bodies, the little ones were wholly destitute of clothing, some of the elders wore blankets. How pleased they were to see the Black-gowns, and how eager that some of the unbaptized should receive the Holy Sacrament of Baptism, for this Sacrament the Indian understands better than any other.

It was curious to see them making bread, kneading it upon their thighs, and baking it in their hastily constructed ovens. A long strange study to watch them, something so far distant from European thought and ways.

But grander was it to hear that prayer taught by the lips of a God man falling from these dusky lips in their own language :

"Intatze ankougtapi manshigta ningshe, shashe dichta
   Father   our   in heaven   who art   Name   thy

ouchoupegtselou, wawalagtankapi dichta tshighselou.
   be hallowed   Kingdom   thy   come

Hakistse ingshe manshingta ekionpi manshan lai
   Will   thy   in heaven   be done ;   on earth   be it

ackougtsiow. Humpale humpake sani wâtsütse ankougtapi
   done likewise.   To-day   and day   every   bread   our

wakupiow. Ouskan pishi wacshiegchepa
   to us give.   Action   bad   to us which has been done

ankionle   ankale   aikon   ouskan   pishi   ankougtapi
 we it   forgive;   so   action   bad   ours

waonlapiow.   Ouskan   pishi   ankagchetapi   wasankapi
 us forgive.   Action   bad   to do by us   lead us

ninkow.   Nansi   pishi   ingshe   walietsi   sapiow. —
 not.   But   evil   from   deliver   us.

Aikougtsiou.
 Amen.

CHAPTER IX.

"I shall be your faithful guide,
Through this gloomy covert wide.
. . . .
                    "And beside,
All the swains that there abide
With jigs and rural dance resort;
We shall catch them at their sport,
And our sudden coming there
Will double all their mirth and cheer."—*Comus.*

THE HUSKING PARTY.

TOM in his everlasting rough knee breeches, knee boots, and his dark cloth shirt—Tom leaning on a potato fork, a basket in one hand filled with sweet potatoes, and those deep-set eyes of his beaming with good humour as he gives to his master's guest an invitation:

"Missis McColl's huskin's on ternight, wants yer and Charley there. Won't yer come? Do now; do now. I'll go with yer. Charley hount. Charley don't like huskins. I does though."

"Hulloa, Tom, what are you talking about, eh?" asks Woodhouse, stopping his writing at the Ranche table.

Tom repeated his message.

"What's a husking, Tom ?   I must know that before I go."

"Wall, I guess yer be ignorant, don't know what a huskin is.   Why yer goes to the house ; yer sits in a barn or outhouse, and yer shells corn, Indian corn ; yer rubs two cobs one agin another ; yer stays two or three hours adoing off that, and then yer goes in the house and yer eats, and the McColls give yer good eating.   Don't know what a huskin be ?   Wall I guess they be funny ones where yer comes from.   Will yer come now, and persuade Charley, too ? "

"I can't promise, Tom, until I know all about it. Tell me, what do you do after supper ? "

"Wall I guess yer bes ignorant.   Yer plays all kind o' games.   Well game, buff game, riggles,[1] all sorts er games."

"Who goes, Tom ? "

"Wall you bes ignorant.   All goes—men, gals, bors ; there us sits, and talks and talks, and works and works. Will yer go, eh ? "

"I must think about it, Tom."

"If Charley goes will yer," asked Tom, returning to the attack, "will yer come with us then ? "

"Yes, I will."

"If he don't go, or is out," and Tom's eyes looked so pleadingly at him ?

---

[1] Riggles = Riddles.

"If he is out I'll go with you, simply as a reward for your persistency, Tom."

"Wall, you bes ignorant; he's a goin to the Upper Ranche after dinner, so yer'll go, and I'll tell McColl this morning;" and with that Tom disappears, saying: "There be the sweet potatoes for dinner; you eats um once, yer won't care for the others."

"Well, I'll busy myself getting dinner, I think. I know Charley will be tired when he comes in, and Tom won't be back awhile, so here goes." And with that the writing ceased. The ashes were knocked out of the pipe, and the preparation began. A prairie chicken to pluck, stuffing to make, the beans and pork to put on the fire to warm up again, and then the peaches to stew and the bread to make, for on the prairies bread has to be made sufficient for the meal only in hot weather.

"Well," said the inhabitant of the Ranche, "if I'm cook they shall feed well for once. I'll make two kinds of bread, corn-bread and flour. Here's a joke. I'm in for it. Well, I remember seeing in an old cookery book, 'How to prepare a hare: Catch him first.' And 'How to cook a dinner: Firstly, light the fire.'"

Very busy was the impromptu cook. The fire in the American oven was burning brightly, the chicken in the oven was browning nicely, and the beans were softening in the pork fat, whilst an appetising savour pervaded the Ranche. The corn-bread was made and ready to go in the oven, and now with sleeves turned up and floury arms, the flour bread was in full swing of making, when the door opened and in came Brown Kirwan.

"Hulloa, Brown, isn't this a joke? I'm cook, and I've got such a jolly dinner on."

"Hulloa, Willie, this is a change. You're a funny Englishman."

"Why, old fellow?"

"Why, just because you've got lots of 'go' in you, and have assimilated yourself to prairie life. 'Zeal,' the old Superior calls it; 'Go,' I call it. How are you getting on here?"

"All right as yet, enjoying myself."

"Where's Charley?"

"He'll be in directly; he's going to the upper Ranche this afternoon."

"Good, so am I; we can go together. I've a patient down already with pleuro-pneumonia."

"Will that epidemic come here, do you think, Brown?" Brown Kirwan got up from his chair, quietly walked to Woodhouse's side, laid his hand upon his shoulder, and quietly said: "It is here already, both spino meningitis and pneumonia."

"Brown!"

"It's true, but you needn't tell the others yet. If you're afraid, go my boy, although I should be deuced sorry to see your back. If you are made of the stuff I take you to be, you will stay and aid the Fathers to nurse the sick. You've got some weeks' breathing time to prepare."

"Brown, can I be of any use?"

"You can, and I believe being fresh from Europe your constitution will be free from the contagion."

"What would you do, were you in my place?"

"If I felt my manhood I should stay. If I felt my cowardice I should go. For one, I depend upon you."

"I think you may do so, Brown."

"What are you two fellows looking so grave about?" asked Charley Kirwan, as his head appeared at one of the windows. "Well, I never. Willie Woodhouse, Willie Woodhouse! Ha, ha, ha. What do you think of that, Brown? An Englishman, a civilized cook on the prairies. We've taught you something, my boy, eh? Oh me, Oh me. Ha, ha, ha! Well, I never. Well, I never."

"Wait till you get your dinner, Charley."

"You'll ruin me, Willie, with that appetising savour, and these hungry Ranche men coming in. Oh, Willie Woodhouse, Willie Woodhouse." And Charley coming in laughed louder than ever, as he took his pipe, and saw, beside the dinner being ready, the hearth swept, and everything in order, even to his pipe being filled for him.

"I say, Brown, I saw a lot of quails about forty feet from the Ranche. Shall we go after them? Won't they cook nice for supper!" And taking his gun the two brothers went out of the Ranche.

In a quarter of an hour, when they returned with eleven quails, the dinner was ready and smoking on the table. The Ranche men also coming in, they sat down a merry party.

"Doc," asked Tom, trying to fix Brown Kirwan's attention.

"Doc are yer coming to the huskin ?"

"Huskin ! Where, Tom ?"

"At McColl's. I said as how Woody and I were going."

"You going, Willie ?" asked Kirwan.

"Yes ; Tom engaged me early this morning."

"Well, I never. Well, I never. Oh me, Oh me," and Charley curled up convulsed on his chair. "Don't play the well game, don't."

"Now who shall I see there, eh ?"

"Well, Deacon McColl, the schoolmaster, the Buttons, and all the people round ; the Wesleyan Minister, too ; perhaps forty."

"Never mind, Willie," said Brown, "Go, it will be a new page of experience opened to you. You would know nothing of the prairies without going to a husking party. One will last you a life-time ; but go and study the Osage Society."

All the food had disappeared from the table, an array of empty plates stood there, the Ranchers had gone, and now the three friends were talking together. Let us listen to their conversation.

"Now, Woodhouse, you study the schools and see if that idea of getting up entertainments is possible. I think you would be surprised to find the latent talent of the prairies hidden under that rough exterior."

The old Superior thought so, too ; he sided with the plan, thinking it showed zeal. "It will be an amusement to you, and a teaching of civilization to your neighbours."

"Imagine Brown, a kind of Penny Reading on the frontier; but *I will* think of it, and study the subjects to-night to see what I can make of them."

"I have a flask of whiskey, and there is some nice hot water, suppose we have a grog with the pipes; a Red Letter Day, as I heard men call feast days in one of the English Universities."

"Now then, friends, come and keep Red Letter Day with me. I'm off to the upper Ranche directly, and for the night too. I'll see and hear of McColl's husking to-morrow, when you will be a wiser man in prairie experience."

"I'm going that way, too, Charley."

"Ah, Brown, but I shall have the ox waggon and my gun."

"In that case I'll drive on in my Buggy, as it's no use waiting for you."

When he had gone, Woodhouse turning to Charley, said: "Do you know, Charley, I believe Brown is down-right ill. I wish you'd ask him to come and stay awhile here, and let me nurse him."

"I think he's more bothered than ill, although he did look white to-day. Poor fellow, he can't get his accounts in, and he's standing at an enormous expense down at the Mission. He has rooms in that place of his over the store, and lives at the Hotel. Then he has horses to keep, &c., &c.; but everybody likes Brown. Brown is such a gentleman. Now I must go. Good bye, old fellow. I shall miss you when you go for good."

As he sat alone in the Ranche, his thoughts ran thus: That epidemic is coming. Well, I shall stand fire. And for these entertainments ? Well, I'll do my best. A useless, idle life brings no pleasure. Pleasure consists in expending one's forces of doing good upon others.

Charley and his brother being well on their journey, a series of visitors arrived. First came the Canadian woman—"short, very thin, and age difficult to tell;" thinner than at her last visit, when Woodhouse first arrived on the prairies. She opened the door as though she belonged to the Ranche. In her sharp, shrill, thin voice she said, "Good day, Woodhus; good day, friend. Charley's not in, eh. I was in hopes he was. I do so want to borrow a cup of coffee kernels ; he'd let me have them if he was at home. Not to home ! Well, I guess I'll take it. Tell him I'll bring it back to-morrow." And she was proceeding to the shelf in high glee to think she had attained her end, when Tom arrived.

"Now then, old 'un. Out yer goes," said Tom. "Enough of that. I saw yer a watching of Charley off. No berries you gits here to-day. Out wid yer, now."

Convulsed with laughing, Woodhouse threw a dollar to her, and a couple of quails. Whereupon she absconded, vowing vengeance against Tom.

Tom, indignant, with mouth wide open, stared at his companion.

"You give to her, do yer, arter she wanted to charge you five dollars for washing that little mess of linen of yours. They're rum uns whar you cum from. We's sharper, we Yanks is."

Hardly had Tom finished speaking when the tall, thin, lantern-jawed form of Levett appeared.

"Be you off to that ere huskin, Woodhus. I be going and my old woman. Now whar be Charley? I want a cup of berries, and a paper of sugar, quick."

"No, Levett," replied Tom, "You cum and ask Charley. True, that be true, the sugar is here in plenty, and the berries too, but they baint ourn; are they, Woodhus?"

Woodhouse nodded.

"Yer don't want um ter-day Levett. Yer cum and ax Charley to-morrow he'll give it, he will I know; but us can't. Can us, Woodhus?"

Again a nod in assent, and then Levett departed; stopping three more intending visitors on his way with the news that Tom was in, and it warn't no go.

"Now, Master Woodhus, I'm goin to saddle the horses, and mind as how you be ready in a few minutes." And whistling some air of his own composition Tom retired, to re-appear with a Texan cob and one of Doc's horses, which he had lent Willie during his stay, and then they were soon galloping towards McColl's Ranche.

Crossing one creek with a made bottom easily, they came to another in which the water looked dark and the stream swollen.

"Now, Mr. Woodhus, you must cross so," and Tom raised his feet and crossed them over his horse's neck, hanging on by the pommel of the Mexican saddle. "You see thus you don't get wet. Hain't Charley taught you to ride like this yet? Oh my, no! Well you watch me cross." And as the water rose high up the saddle Tom escaped dry as possible. " Be careful now, cos it ull be dangerous at night if you ain't pertickler." Closely following Tom's teaching, and the horse being used to the crossing, they both landed safely on the other side. " Now, Mr. Woodhus, you would hardly believe it, but that 'ere crick rises ten feet sometimes, and with a skitty horse its dangerous then. But McColl's huskin's begun. Gee-up, hos, and away we goes."

Arrived at McColl's—one of the better class of houses, with some pretension of furniture about it, and three rooms at the least, besides kitchen—they found a great company congregated ; girls with smart ribbons, men with their best coats on, and even old ladies, busy in the barn (a good-sized barn too, that of McColl's) sitting in a circle round a rapidly-growing heap of maize. There was order, too, in the arrangement. Some appointed to supply them with cobs, from which the huskers pulled the husks, and then rubbing two cobs together the grain fell in rich, golden profusion on to the great heap near which they were sitting ; and all the time whilst hands worked hard, tongues worked harder. There was McColl with his two sons and two daughters, his man and the Schoolmaster, a young fellow of eighteen ; there was Button and his family, and a gathering of unknown Ranchers. Tom's arrival was welcome, for Tom was a famed husker, and Woodhouse was placed between McColl and a Miss Dempsey, a school-mistress of an adjoining district. McColl, or Deacon McColl, was a long man with a Gladstonian face, an Ohio man, not without cleverness, and generally with more cultivation than his neighbours. Miss Dempsey was a Texan woman of three-and-twenty, or more, gentle and lady-like, a born sister of charity living in the world. Where sickness was found, there shadow-like and un-assuming stood Anna Dempsey ; where sorrow was, there tracing quick upon sorrow's heel came Anna Dempsey, a comfortress indeed. The district in which stood Miss Dempsey's school was one in which order reigned near disorder. People wondered how she rendered so tractable those rough specimens who came to her up to seventeen years of age. She was not a pretty woman ; she dressed in that quiet grave way that became the face, on which sometimes played that pure light and smile one catches on the face of the best type of Murillo's angels ; her hair was brushed smoothly, in some way peculiar to herself, away from her face ; looking at her you forgot she had not a tall handsome figure ; the expression of her face was all to her. She sat, in her way, upon a kind of throne, before which the prairie people did homage, unknowingly to herself, unknowingly to themselves.

"Is Charley coming, Mr. Woodhouse ? " asked McColl.

" I don't think so, Mr. McColl," answered Woodhouse, fighting desperately with an obstinate cob which would not yield its corn. " He is at the upper Ranche."

" And Doc ? "

" Oh, he's out in the same direction ; gone to see some obstinate case of pleuro pneumonia."

" Ah," observed Mr. McColl, " The Lord will chastise His people."

Those quick, eager eyes of Miss Dempsey were raised to Woodhouse's face. " Does Doc think we shall get the epidemic amongst us ? "

" I can't answer that question, Miss Dempsey ; it seems to me it is coming nearer to us."

" And are *you* going, Sir ?

" No, I think not, Miss Dempsey, not if I am wanted."

The deep voice of the Deacon addressed them both. " They all forsook Him and fled. You won't flee with those cowardly disciples, and leave only the weak women standing by the Cross ? "

" I hope I shall be able to remain, Mr. McColl."

" Ah, you don't know what illness is on the prairie, when a man's alone, laid on his bed, no fire, no one to prepare his food, no one to attend his cattle ; why, I've opened a Ranche door before now and found the owner dead on his bed through neglect ; but the Lord did it, the Lord did it, and for some wise purpose, surely."

" Mr. McColl, we want some more cobs."

" You'll find a rick full in the yard ; bring 'em in boys."

The company were soon supplied again with work, and the laugh and jest went round, and right merrily did they quaff the Deacon's wine and ale, home-brewed foaming ale, a treat to all.

" Miss Dempsey, I am coming round to see your school one of these days ; I hear it is a model one."

" I shall be pleased to show it you," was the quiet answer.

" Don't you think this winter we might possibly get

up some entertainments in the school-houses for the people ? "

" What kind of entertainments ? "

" Well, what in Europe we call ' Penny Readings.' We have glees, comic or serio-comic readings, one or two short instructive pieces of natural history, a song or so, and then wind up with the National Anthem."

" Well, that is capital, Mr. Woodhouse ; if you will arrange for the Readings, I will get up the glees and songs ; my children are not behind-hand in music ; I only want a week's preparation."

It was rapidly growing dusk now, and the Deacon hurried up his guests by assuring them " No work, no play," and so with an energy the husking went on, until the last cob fell from the hands of Tom. Then came a moving of seats, a greater buzz of conversation, cheers from the young men, and an adjournment to the house was proposed, where Mrs. McColl was discovered busy with the supper preparation. Mrs. McColl was a superior woman, a widow whom the Deacon had wooed and won in some western city. The table was well laid out, and to the astonishment of some, adorned with solid silver cruets and spoons, and large bouquets of flowers. A large turkey flanked one end—smoking hot ; then when one tired of that sight, one saw ducks and fowls temptingly arranged as side dishes. A large ham also smoked invitingly near the Deacon ; then blanc-manges, nestling in cranberry jam, and jellies nodded to the company ; and as a centrepiece stood an enormous cake.

How Tom's eyes sparkled—nay, nearly all the eyes in that over-hungry company.

Mrs. McColl, who had her stranger guest near her, enjoyed his surprise :

"You wonder civilisation has touched upon this border life, so close to the Osages, eh, Mr. Woodhouse ? Ah well, sir ; misfortune has introduced me to strange companions."

It was Miss Dempsey who saw unshed tears in Mrs. McColl's eyes ; and she, sitting on the other side of her Hostess, gently pressed her hand. It seemed indeed a mystery that those two women's hearts could take in and slave for those of that company.

A quiet lesson was growing into the soul of Willie Woodhouse ; he knew that on that strange border-land many beautiful lives were being lived, and over them, and upon their grand souls was resting the light of purity and holiness—all growing from those words : "Inasmuch as ye did it unto one of the least of these my brethren, ye did it unto Me."

"You may not like the games afterwards ; *we do not,* but as it is *the custom* we tolerate them ;" and Mrs. McColl sighed.

I would my space allowed me to detail all that supper conversation on the Indians and their ways ; of the last murders near Independence ; of the epidemic spread far and wide in Kansas territory ; of the last wedding, and the wedding guests ; and the last riddle in circulation (riggles Tom called them). And now the table cleared by willing hands, and the table itself quickly stowed in an out-of-the-way corner, a wild scene commences. Blind man's buff, in which even the Deacon joins amidst screams of laughter—keen enjoyment such as those who live in that prairie world can appreciate, for such meetings as these are few and rare.

And then came the "Well game," at which many declined to play. It consisted in one person going into a corner and proclaiming himself in a well. "Who is to pull you out?" "So-and-so." "How deep are you down?" "Ten feet;" and each foot represented a kiss. Then the puller out was in a well, and the same thing was acted over again until all those playing were in a long line across the room, and the depths grew marvellously—and the laughter too.

Here the Deacon broke up the game by introducing pipes and spirits; and Woodhouse, who had been talking with the Deacon, prevailed on Tom to get the horses. In a few minutes they were riding over the dark prairie, and the Husking party with its kaleidoscopic scenes was of the past.

CHAPTER X.

"In his lodge beside a river,
Close beside a frozen river.

*   *   *   *

Seeing nothing but the snow-storm
As it whirled, and hissed, and drifted."—
From " Hiawatha."—Longfellow.

SUNSET AND SNOW-STORM.

THE unusually long Indian summer was about to close, the quiet beautiful days were waning into winter, and those whose business brought them in contact with the Indians were saying that an unusually rigorous winter was to be anticipated, and indeed was prophesied by all the tribes. Fell *pleuropneumonia* and *spino-meningitis* were creeping nearer and nearer to the Mission.

Charley Kirwan had an artist's soul within him. For some days he had been promising his guest to show him a prairie sunset—such a sunset that he might take back to Europe, hidden away in his memory, and gloat over ever after. On this afternoon they rode away into the broad prairie, and waited, watching the western sky. There was no sentimentality in this, nought was farther from Kirwan's mind ; but he wished to give an idea of what nature's color-painting was like.

The heavens all around them were clear deep blue, excepting to the westwards, where lay one long bank of snowy cloud ; almost imperceptibly the snowy mass was stained with crimson, which grew intense in its coloring ; gradually glintings of gold stole into the crimson, each color deepening in strength and beauty ; then the glory was of crimson, purple, and gold seeemingly reflected in the tall prairie grass. For a few moments the beauty was great as it gradually approached its zenith. Those looking on felt themselves bathed in color ; but there came a purple haze over that fair glory and it was night. Yes, night and silence ; time and the insect noises round them seemed swallowed in that still sea of mist rising up from the earth.

No words passed between the friends—words seemed almost blasphemous in face of that still prairie, and the wondrous painting whose beauty had grown into their souls. It seemed so fresh from the hands of God, with nothing to stain its purity. And thus ended the Indian summer for Willie Woodhouse.

Later on in the evening Charley Kirwan was speaking of sunsets in the Bay of Naples, and comparing them with sunsets in the West thus : " Of course they have been sung and written about almost to excess ; whilst our sunsets in the Bay of New York and on these great plains are comparatively little known. I certainly prefer our own sunsets ; they are on such a vaster scale, and the coloring seems more intense, and one feels them more because darkness follows so quickly on all the brilliant coloring."

I have described elsewhere the lean-to bedroom occupied by Kirwan and his guest, and described the eventful chinks unmortared where it joined on to the Ranche proper. A few days after they studied the prairie sunset, Charley Kirwan, being awake first, called to his companion to open his eyes. During the night there had been a great fall of snow, and it had drifted through the inch-and-a-half or two-inch chink between the lean-to and the Ranche. Their bedroom was literally carpetted with snow—it had even drifted on to the coverlet, and its soft fleecy ridges lay about the bed. Dreamily Woodhouse awoke and glanced round. Had he gone to sleep in a snow-drift ? and then, as the ludicrosity of the scene burst upon the senses, came prolonged peals of laughter from both of them. It was such a hunt to find their clothing—here in a miniature snow bank lay slippers ; there in a snow bank was discovered a vest ; and in the meanwhile outside the window could nothing be seen " but the snowstorm, as it whirled, and hissed, and drifted."

" Oh, Charley : how odd this is."

" Odd ; I told you the winter would be as quickly upon us as the sunset faded the other night."

There was somewhat of silence until Kirwan said :

" Another experience of prairie life for you ; your education will be nearer finished when you get back to Europe."

"I am not surprised you like the prairies, Charley, there is something fascinating about these sudden changes."

"Not more sudden than the transit from life to death, Woodhouse ; " and there crept into his tone that yearning earnestness which was one of his great fascinations.

" Sharley—Sharley ; I say, where's Sharley," and the voice of Lieboldt reached through the closed door. " A wintry mornin', Sharley ; but I want Sharley. I say to the boys, they cattle be fed under the trees—the snow fall he hide the hay—the cattle no find he ; " and opening the door communicating with the lean-to—the shock head and good-natured face of the German appeared in the opening. His astonishment was the cause of prolonged laughter. But Lieboldt was no man of straw. With broom and energy he soon expelled the intruding snow, laughing the while.

CHAPTER XI.

"Be this, then, a lesson to thy soul, that thou reckon nothing
    worthless,
"Because thou heedest not its use, nor knowest the virtues
    thereof."

PENNY READINGS ON THE PRAIRIES.

IN these wintry days the schools on the Prairies were in full operation. Unlike English schools, for the working youth laid aside his calling and became a school-boy again in these winter months; the tall girls of eighteen and twenty, thirsting for knowledge, brought up to the School House their little brothers and sisters and stayed to be taught themselves; and the big young men brought their brothers and sisters, and all worked with a will under the guidance of some Schoolmaster or Schoolmistress. I think in the laying-out of the counties there is ground allowed for the building of a School House in each half-mile, or square mile. In the summer months the schools are closed, and in the winter months filled to excess. It seems difficult to find out where the people come from.

Tom, who through the kindness of Kirwan, was

attending the schools, and yet staying on at the Ranche, had taken Woodhouse with him to the evening schools, and many a long discussion was held between the stranger and the Schoolmasters or Mistresses as to the entertainments to be given.

It was thus that the idea of giving these entertainments arose :

After the night-school was over, the pupils, young and old, set to and had a regular romp, in which often the " well game " was prominent.   Now if one could only utilize these half-hours by getting up some Entertainments, and induce the performers to devote this half-hour to preparing for them, much good might be done.

Miss Dempsey was enlisted speedily, and already the singing class, picked from her school, was practising glees and solos.   One of the Doctors from the Mission was invited to give a short lecture on Education, in language the people could understand.   Willie Woodhouse was to give a lecture on " Horace Greeley's Prairie Life "; whilst an Irishman from a distant Ranche was to bring his violin and sing some of Tom Moore's melodies, accompanying himself ; but certain young people, who *could not sing* and *who would not read*, insisted on a play.

Miss Dempsey being consulted, in her quiet way replied, " Why not let them have a ' Tableaux ' ? "

" An excellent idea," chorused the Committee, " because then they must be silent."

Thus it was decided. The entrance fee to the entertainment was to be a quarter of a dollar ; but a deputation came in on the day of the Reading itself, to say many Ranchers would like to come who had no " quarters " ; who had, in fact, no money whatever, but who would gladly pay in kind.

" Let them all come," said Woodhouse, " we want a good audience."

Charley Kirwan chaffed about the energy displayed in the movement ; but, nevertheless, the interest in it grew and grew, until on the night itself, the collection of strange vehicles round the Prairie School-House was encouraging indeed.

But where to seat all the people—if one could only stretch those wooden walls out farther.

So, the English Penny Readings were introduced on the distant Osage Prairies of the Far West. I query if the founder of these entertainments thought they would reach so far.

A few minutes' explanation to the Prairie gathering of settlers, then came a glee—enthusiastically received —and the Doctor's Lecture, well put together, and fit for that strange assembly ; he knew how to touch gently the heart's core of such an audience, and awake their finer feelings. The first tableau succeeded to the the lecture.

It was " Faith." We heard the silence grow in the room before the wonderful still beauty of her face. And yet it was only Barbara Mackintosh, whose brown plebeian hands were whitened that they might not offend the audience. Before God though, methinks oft times those brown hands reached higher than white ones.

Then came the Goddess of Liberty, in a beautiful American flag. We watched to see Zenobia's chains in order before she posed herself. All remembered that tableau for days after. Some latent instinct of heroism was astir in that girl's blood. For a moment the girl went away from herself. She was thrilled with a deep sense of power that will last longer than that deep prolonged applause from Ranchemen's throats.

Was it not a little like life? We, who were behind the curtain; we, looking on that wrong side, saw all the mistakes, all the loose threads and thrums. And yet perhaps, if we could look on the other side we should see how honest faith and earnest endeavour have woven a pattern fit for a king's robe. Behind the curtain, hurry, confusion, chaos; before the curtain, a fair vision of men and women.

Can it be true that we do not give the right meaning to success and failure in life? Is what we call success always really worthy of the name?

The one perfect life that has been lived on earth from a merely human point of view was a *failure*. It had neither wealth, nor riches, nor fame. It went swiftly down to a sudden, terrible death, embittered by cruel mockery. Yet who questions that it was the one successful complete life; this highest thought of God, uttered in humanity?

7

The Horace Greeley lecture came next, and was followed by songs, glees, and a comic reading.

In the meanwhile new life was stealing over the faces of the audience. The hard lines of care loosened into something gentler, and mayhaps some vision of the days of childhood grew up in the men's hearts, and women's also.

Well pleased they went to their ox waggons and mounted their Texan cobs for their cold prairie ride home to their cheerless Ranches.

But the young men grouped together were holding some discussion with Kirwan's friend about the epidemic; —they were forming themselves into a nursing committee to nurse any sick in their district during the nights when their own farm work was done.

And this grew out of the Penny Readings on the Prairies. In the meanwhile, Miss Dempsey was making some proposition to the young women to take the day nursing; and so they looked to their armour to prepare for the enemy, and, as the sequel will show, it was well they did so.

Very happy, indeed, was the thought of these Prairie Entertainments; and all honor be to him who introduced Penny Readings into England — for from England they have been carried into many Countries, and amongst many Peoples.

The next day Brown Kirwan came to stay at the Ranche, and took Woodhouse and Tom fishing on the frozen creek. They skated, and thus followed the fish easier. Brown looked carefully at the fish crowding under the ice, and fixing on a fine red mullet-looking fellow, brought down the axe with a thud upon the ice over the fish's head. The fish lay motionless under the ice, stunned. Then with a dexterity that would surprise a European, he gently cut the ice in a square about the fish just wide enough to insert the sieve (Tom carried) under the body of the victim. In a few minutes it lay kicking in the basket, having recovered from the effects of the blow immediately it was exposed to the air. Soon the basket Woodhouse carried grew heavy ; but still he insisted on fishing out odd specimens of fish — especially one with a body almost like a pike and a beak like a duck. And a good fish dinner rewarded them for their exertions. How pleasant it was on the Creek—winter fishing, the great trees on either side shutting it in, and the snowy outline tracery on the over-hanging branches forming a continuous triumphal arch.

Even Tom looked up and said it was beautiful.

It was a fair dream of winter beauty. One such a scene that imprints itself on the pages of memory's album, and startles the beholder as he turns the leaves, to think that he has lived in it—has himself felt it.

CHAPTER XII.

"And now the stream has reached
  A dark deep sea ;
And sorrow, dim and crowned
  Is waiting thee.
*   *   *   *   *
Then, with slow reverend step,
  And beating heart,
From out thy joyous days,
  Thou must depart."—*A. Proctor.*

THOSE SAD DAYS.

BROWN KIRWAN lately had taken up his quarters at the Ranche for good. It was easy to see by the attenuation of his form, and the light that burnt in his eyes, and that wan look upon his cheeks, that a great sweet voice had already whispered in his ears : "Friend, come up higher." And Brown Kirwan had lowly bowed his head and gone to the prairie Ranche to prepare for the inevitable.

Willie Woodhouse was his nurse, although in the rough Ranche it was difficult indeed to do all that one could wish ; yet it was possible to get him little delicacies now and again—a quail on toast, the breast of a prairie chicken, some stewed peaches. All these little attentions it was out of the question for the Ranche boys to give, as they were away at their work, excepting for a few minutes in the middle of the day, when they came in tired, yet noisy, to their dinner.

And in these days a deeper affection sprang up between those two who spent so many hours together.

"Now, Brown; I'm going to make you a beautiful dinner before the others come in."

"No you shall not, Willie; you are tired out already."

"Tired out, Brown Kirwan?"

"Well, please don't trouble about me."

"Don't trouble about me, eh Brown; and for how much do you count Jesus Christ, whom I honor in your person?"

Brown Kirwan said no more, but those great eyes of his were eloquent with thanks.

"Do you think I am very ill?"

"I think so, Brown; and I want you to be baptized."

"Does Charley know how ill I am?"

"I can't say; he has been absent a good deal lately at the upper Ranche—he has said nothing to me."

"I shall try to tell him. I should not like him to come home and find me dead."

"Let us hope, Brown, God will give you a longer time to make that solemn preparation for death."

"I don't think so—I know my constitution; I shall go on right to the end. I shall burn away gradually as a candle does, and the last flicker will disappear with a dash-up at the old brilliancy."

"Brown!"

"And I feel, Willie, it is near the last flicker."

"Would you like to see the Old Superior, or any of the Fathers, Brown?"

"I don't know. One thing I do know, I am satisfied with Him whom I have trusted that He will not desert me at that great and awful hour. I thank Him for sending you to me, Willie Woodhouse—I thank Him. I sometimes think that dream may yet be realised."

"Oh, Brown;" and then he laid his head upon his hands, and great sobs shook his frame, whilst burning drops fell through his fingers on to the floor.

"You will tell Charles, and my mother and father, when I am gone, that I tried to love God, and to serve Him, in serving my fellow-men."

And so Brown Kirwan broke the news of his illness to his friend.

Levett coming in to see "Doc," as he called the Doctor, interrupted their quiet chat, and the preparation for dinner left no time for Woodhouse to join in their conversation.

And now on all sides from the Ranchers' homes came wails of sorrow, for scarcely anyone but had some friend down with pleuro-pneumonia or spino-meningitis. The nursing committee was thoroughly organized ; and although Woodhouse disliked leaving the Doctor, yet he felt it was incumbent on him to go out and take his turn at night nursing.

And here I may state the way in which this spino-meningitis is doctored, to show how tedious is the nursing ; and I have known one case to last for ninety days, and yet at last the patient died, in spite of all care lavished upon him. On the first appearance of the disease the spine is blistered the entire length, and then hot white leaves of cabbage, boiled, applied constantly every half hour, or hour, to keep the blistered part open, and make it draw well.

And thus it was difficult and restless nursing ; more so when, as generally was the case, it was necessary to instruct the sick persons in all the truths of Christianity, and prepare' them for the Sacraments.

To baptize some of them—and a consolation it was to think their souls appeared before their Maker with the bright baptismal drops still glittering upon their brows. A beauteous crown indeed, wherewith to go up crownèd, into that crownèd Presence, baptized with water and the Holy Ghost.

Tom came rushing in breathless from his work the next morning, to Woodhouse : "It's little Ike as is dying now ; they want yer quick. The old man's heard as yer can nus a bit. Sez I : 'he's a busy, and bin up all night.' 'Never mind,' says he, 'Tell him its a father's prayer, and Ike won't recuperate again.' I know'd yer'd go,' so the mare is saddled at the door. I'm off, as Charley's busy a helping of us."

Mounting the mare, Woodhouse rode off rapidly in the direction of Nathan Higgin's Ranche — difficult travelling, too, with the snow about. Going gently along at one time, in what he thought was the path covered with snow, the mare disappeared under him, and he found himself sinking in the snow, until only his head remained above the surface. At another time he would have laughed and enjoyed such a state of affairs; but now, with "that sorrow dim awaiting him," it was a different state of things. Getting out of the drift himself, and gently pulling the reins—the mare, used to such circumstances, quietly turned round and came out of the drift. Without much trouble, beyond this, he arrived at the Ranche.

None of the order prevailing in an English sick-room was there, for, according to frontier etiquette, whenever a person was ill, there one found all his friends around him—sometimes to the number of ten or twelve; and the Hostess, if there be one, occupied in cooking for visitors, instead of being able to give her undivided attention to the invalid.

Such was the case now, and the poor child Ike, worn out with the excitement of seeing new faces, and hearing his state so much discussed in his presence, was even then entering into his agony. Gasping for breath— and the very air kept from him by the well-meaning crowd around his bed—his poor dying eyes brightened up when Woodhouse entered, making his way noiselessly through the one-roomed Ranche, which, though larger than the ordinary Ranches, was not built for such a crowded audience. He sat down on the bed-head, and lifted the poor dying little body, placing his arm under the pillow, to give more ease to the sufferer.

"Ike, little Ike; do you know me ?"

A glad smile came over the wan face, and from his panting lips came the words :

"Ike's going to Jesus. Ike's going to the beautiful country."

Moistening his lips with water, Woodhouse asked :

"And is Ike glad ?"

"Oh, Mr. Willie; Ike is glad to go to God. Ike will be an Angel, and sing to Him. Ike will see the Holy Babies—(the Innocents)—the bad king killed, and play with them."

"And won't you think of us, Ike, when you are there ; of your father and mother, and of all of us ?"

"Yes ; every day I will ask God to give you good things ; and I know He will, because I'll say 'for Jesus Christ's sake,' and I'll look to where Jesus Christ stands. He says the little children may go to Him, and God won't say NO to what we ask in His Name."

Tears were coursing down the cheeks of the people present, and yet the little child spoke on the words God gave him.

"Ike will see Mary, too."

"Yes ; Ike will see Mary, the Mother of Jesus."

"And Ike will love her, because there was 'no room for her in the Inn' you told me of; but there's room for her in God's palace, cos she's God's Mother. Perhaps she'll be my mother; and I'll call her mother till my mother comes to me."

"Try to sleep, Ike;" and Woodhouse motioned the people to go still farther away. "Try to sleep, Ike."

"Sleep when God wants me. No; I can't sleep," said the excited child. "Will God have any one there to play with me, and make me playthings?"

"Yes; He will have an harp for Ike, and Ike will hear music like the Angels sang to the Shepherds. You remember the Shepherds, and the concert in the air, Ike, when Christ was born?"

"Yes; I remember. Ike remembers. The Angels carried the poor man's soul to God's palace. Ike remembers: 'Hail Mary, full of Grace, the Lord is with thee.' God's with her—you told me so; she's with God, too. Ike wants to go to his new mother."

And now exhausted, the tired child sank to sleep. Still Woodhouse moved not his arm away from under the pillow for fear of waking the sufferer, and only did he yield his post to Miss Dempsey, who came in when her school hours were finished.

Then, tired to death almost, he rolled himself up in a rug; and, in spite of the dogs of the Ranche persistently walking over him, in a short time was in a profound sleep. He was awakened in the early morning to say the "Prayers for the dying;" and there in the early morning light, from the arms of Willie Woodhouse, Angels carried Ike to God's palace; and now he calls Mary his mother.

Little Angel Ike, what must be thy surprise, having gone from that clumsy Ranche, to find thyself in that finished building—that Palace of the Great King. How sweet thy grateful look of loving surprise must have been even to thy God.

With weeping, the body of Ike was laid out upon a form—the little body that had seen but ten summers, and Nathan Higgins started for the Mission to buy his child a coffin. Willie Woodhouse accompanied him. The Superior, seeing Woodhouse looking ill himself, insisted on keeping him there for that day and night, and promised to let him go up to the Ranche again for a day before the Feast of Christmas.

"How is Doc?" *

"Very sadly."

"Ah; so I thought. I will return with you to see him; I wish very much to baptize him before he dies. And now you, go rest in your room, you will find a fire there."

And to the room he went, and found a fire, two bedsteads, a tub for a washhand-stand, a tin basin, and some frozen water.

And right well did he sleep, the sleep of exhaustion, which was to refresh him for many nights to come.

---

* Doc. Abbreviation of Doctor, commonly in use in the Western States.

CHAPTER XIII.

> " O the long and dreary winter,
>   O the cold and cruel winter ;
>   Ever thicker, thicker, thicker,
>   Froze the ice on lake and river ;
>   Ever deeper, deeper, deeper,
>   Fell the snow o'er all the landscape,
>   Fell the covering snow and drifted."
>   *" Hiawatha."—Longfellow.*

THE DOCTOR'S DEATH.

SO profoundly Willie Woodhouse slept, that the Superior knocked several times at his door the following morning before he could awaken him to come and assist at the last Mass in the Church. A strong east wind blew from the Prairies, and seemed to freeze the very marrow in one's bones, even in crossing the little distance between the House and the Church. The icy wind seemed to penetrate everywhere. It gained so much force in the great breadth of Prairie over which it travelled, that when it came in contact with an object it seemed impatient to level it with the ground. But the Superior had tasted of the east wind before he built his

Church, and there the east wind was mastered, as it could not fell the long, low, stout-built building. How the wind shrieked round the corners, and beat against the few windows, and rushed in through any unwary cranny or ventilator. The Lay-brothers wrapped their coats closer round them, and the Priests their cloaks ; whilst the few people in the Church at that early hour hurried off as soon as the last Gospel was read.

As they sat in the bare Refectory over their breakfast, the Superior said, " You won't go up to the Ranche in this freezing wind, Mr. Woodhouse ? "

" I must, for two reasons—Charley expects me, and the Doctor is really so ill I felt unwilling to leave him yesterday."

" But you will be frozen."

" Never mind, I shall perish in doing my duty."

" Tut, tut : you can't go in the teeth of such a wind, you would be getting your ears frozen, or else your knees, and have to get down to rub your face, ears, and knees with snow twenty times on such a journey. No, you can't go ; those are my orders that you rest here."

" Well, we shall see how it is at mid-day."

" Yes, WE *will see*," replied the old man, as he toddled off after his day's work. " You must amuse yourself in the Library, and about in the Mission as best you can, for I'm busy this morning until dinner."

Left to himself, he wandered into the Library, a

square building, built apart from the rest of the Houses, with a spacious room above it for distribution of prizes to the school, school examinations, &c., &c. He found the priest Quinlin there, and consequently sat down to chat with him.

"I wanted to see you, Father Quinlin, for the other day I came across an Irish couple on the Prairies, living without the Sacrament of Matrimony. I told them *they must renew their consent before a Priest*, and receive the Nuptial Blessing. They are willing to do so publicly; but I suggested that it should be privately done, as the world at large, otherwise, would be cognisant of the affair. They are quite willing to suffer for their fault if they can be an example to others in their state. I said this was not required."

"All, well, my boy," observed the priest, "I will be there as soon as this east wind ceases."

"Yes, and at the same place there is a child to be baptized, about six years of age."

"All, well, my boy; all well. I will see to it. You work stedfastly according to your state in the work of the Minor Orders of the Church, and may God's blessing go with you."

"Are you tired with this Prairie life now the epidemic has come among us?" enquired the Priest after a pause.

"Oh, no. It gives one all the more zest to stay where one can find work to one's hand."

"The zeal of Thine House hath eaten me up, O Lord." "Zelus domus tuæ comedit me."

" By the way, I want to ask you about the Convent. What Order have you there ? "

" The Lorettines, or the Sisters of Loretto ; some people call them 'The Friends of Mary at the foot of the Cross.' "

" I've never heard anything about them, excepting here."

" I daresay not ; they were established in the Diocese of Kentucky by a Father Nerinckx."

" Who was he ? "

" A Belgian, born in 1761, who came to the United States at the age of forty-five, and was sent into Kentucky by Bishop Carroll, who then, under Pius the VI., had jurisdiction over the whole of the United States."

" What kind of reputation did he leave behind him ? I mean Nerinckx."

" Well, he erected ten Churches in Kentucky—two of them brick Churches, the others of hewed logs—he always helped the workmen at their work, whilst they were cutting the timber, or clearing out the under-growth."

" Did he do anything else ? "

" Yes, he had charge of six large congregations, and a greater number of stations scattered about over the whole of Kentucky. He founded this Sisterhood in 1812, and in twelve years from its commencement the number of Sisters exceeded a hundred."

" And how many schools had they under them then ? "

"Six different schools for girls. They were then educating about 250 girls."

"Well, but Father Quinlin, how came they here?"

"In this way; we succeeded so well with the education of the Indian boys, that the Indian Chiefs of the Osage tribe came and demanded us to educate the girls; and then the Father Superior resolved to interest some fervent community of Nuns in the education of Osage girls."

"Well?"

"Well, he went to S. Louis with this intention, applied to several convents to undertake this work, but they were all frightened at the magnitude of it, until he asked the good sisters of Loretto."

"And when did they come?"

"In 1847. Four of them came; and many privations they have had to put up with before they inhabited the House you see them in now."

"And now they have twenty sisters here?"

"Yes, twenty sisters now."

"Well, having asked you all this, I want you to take me to see over the Convent and the Schools."

"I was waiting for that demand to come, and I accede to it as far as I can. You will be surprised to hear some of their rules; one thing they have to do is to dig a spadeful of earth out of their grave every day, to remind them of death. I shan't be able to go over the Convent with you to-day, but some other time I promise to do so."

"I shall have a rough sort of ride up to Kirwan's Ranche in this wild wind, shan't I, Father Quinlin?"

"Aye my boy; you can't go."

"Well, I have made up my mind to go, unless I hear Brown Kirwan is better."

"Brown Kirwan will never be better this side of the grave; I saw him walking to visit a patient in the Mission some week or so ago, and I was grieved to my heart's core to notice what a wreck he had become."

"And nothing can be done for him; and you would leave him out in that lonely old Ranche to die unbaptized? No, Father Quinlin, I can't tolerate that."

"Impulsive as ever. Can you baptize the man against his will?"

"No; but by gentleness, patience, logic, I would convince his will, that unless he is baptized of water and the Holy Ghost he cannot enter into the kingdom of heaven."

"Well, but there are two other kinds of Baptism, that of *desire*, and that of *blood*. If he dies with the strong desire for that Sacrament, and there is no one by to administer it, then that desire before God counts as though the Sacrament had been validly administered by a lawfully appointed minister."

"But that is so unsatisfactory to look back upon. One is not sure."

"We never know what acts go on in a soul at its last moment, what voiceless acts of sorrow and love go out from the stricken spirit to the feet of Christ, and God is always more anxious for men's salvation than we are."

"Yes, that's very true; but, I should like Brown to be baptized; he is so morally good, there is something so genuine about him."

"Leave him in God's hands, my son, in God's hands."

That day after the conversation with the Fathers, Woodhouse had made up his mind to do what they thought best, and not brave a ride in the wind, as it then blew as fiercely as ever. The morning began to lay on his hands, and an unquiet feeling arose in his mind that he must go. So saddling his horse, and wrapping his furs about him, he went to the Superior.

"I can't rest here, Father. I feel something urging me out to Kirwan's Ranche—something that won't admit of delay. I know for certitude Brown Kirwan is dying."

There was such an earnestness in his tone, that the Superior merely said:

"God's blessing and protection go with you. With a feeling like that upon you I won't bid you stay."

Quickly mounting his horse, he was trotting sharply on his road to the Prairie. How fiercely the wind blew for some time he was unconscious; the wind as it blew against him seemed to shriek: "Brown Kirwan is dying;" and by some inner acquiescence of his own spirit he felt this was true.

And now, on the broad Prairie, without the protection

of the trees growing upon the banks of the creek, the wind blew more icily keen, and seemed to go down into his very marrow. If only he could reach the Ranche, though. Yet he felt his knees stiffening with the cold, and his ears seemed hard and stiff, as though frozen.

Horrid stories floated through his brain, of people on this self-same Prairie who had had their ears so frozen that as they touched them they broke off. Could this be true, or was it some hoax told to him? The deadly numbness creeping through his knees warned him that he must get off and rub them with snow unless he would be frost-bitten; so pulling up his horse, and dismounting, he rubbed his ears, his knees, and his hands with snow until the circulation returned; and, once again wrapping his furs closely around him, started afresh on his journey, the conviction all the while growing more strongly upon him that Brown Kirwan was dying.

In that journey, in the teeth of an east wind, three times did he repeat the operation of rubbing himself with snow to keep the life within him, thus saving himself, as that numbness and sleepiness were creeping over him, from death by freezing. Desolate enough looked the wide snowy waste, as ridge after ridge of prairie extended before him. And now his journey bordering on to the creek again, he stopped at a low Ranche, hidden away in the outskirt wood of the creek, to give the message to these Irish people concerning the subject on which he had spoken to Quinlin in the morning—that was of their Marriage, and their renewal

of consent before a Minister of God. Having finished
his mission, and hastily swallowed some hot coffee to
warm him, he was about to proceed upon his journey,
when the man asked him—

"How's Doc Kirwan? I asks, 'cos I see Doc Seagrim
from the Mission, gallop rapidly by a short time ago, in
the direction of Kirwan's Ranche?"

"I don't know how he is now; I haven't seen him
for two days, but I think he's very ill indeed."

"Ah, poor dear Doc, he won't recuperate," chimed
in the man's wife; and the little child of six, hearing
the parents talking thus, lisped out: "Poor Doc."

"I guess as how he's worse," rejoined the man,
"mayhap a dying."

By the time he had finished this remark, his recent
auditor was galloping away as fast as his horse could
carry him. Through the snow-covered brush-wood
nearing the creek, on over another stretch of prairie,
then came Kirwan's Ranche in sight; and there at
the door, by straining his eyes, he could make out a
strange horse. "Doctor Seagrim is there; now I must
haste to hear the news."

Reining up at the Ranche door, and breathlessly
throwing the reins to Tom, who held the Doctor's horse,
he motioned to Tom to tell him the news.

Tom turned away, and a great tear rolled down his
cheek; but making a step forward, with his huge hand
he clutched the hand of Woodhouse as if to detain him
from entering the Ranche.

"Tom, leave go ; I must see him."

Tom tried to speak, and with tears bursting from his eyes, huskily muttered :

"Doc's just dead."

What a sight met his eyes as he opened the Ranche door. The wood fire flame flickered, and crept softly about the great stone hearth. A bed was drawn almost in front of it, and on the bed lay Brown Kirwan, sunk deep in that dreamless sleep from which neither human love nor hate shall awake him more. He was fully dressed, and wrapped in his heavy great coat ; and by his side stood Charles Kirwan, as though carved in stone, and by Charles Kirwan stood the Doctor Seagrim.

"He cannot be dead, Dr. Seagrim. It must be a fainting fit."

"No, he is dead, Mr. Woodhouse," replied the Doctor, touching the pulse through which the crimson blood would pulsate never more.

Charley Kirwan felt an arm laid kindly upon his own ; and through the still Ranche the words resounded, "Let us pray."

And then three men were kneeling.

Gradually that statuesque look passed off Charley Kiwan's face, and warm tears rolled from under his closed eyelids. Until then he heeded not the wind shrieking around the corners of the Ranche, crying wildly for mercy. Mayhap a wilder tempest was raging in his own soul ; but blessed feet have walked upon the waves of this troublesome life, and ever when rightly sought does a diviner voice assuage life's tumult ; and now as eighteen hundred years. ago, when HE saith "Peace, be still," there is a great calm.

As they rose from their knees Dr. Seagrim spoke ;—"We must lay him out, or he will be frozen in that posture."

Gently and kindly were the last offices performed by kind hearts, and rough hands, under the direction of Woodhouse ; for Charley Kirwan had stolen away—*that* sight he could not bear.

In the Ranche, in a short hour, everything had resumed its ordinary shape — excepting for that still form lying under the white sheet upon the bed in the corner.   They could not put the corpse in. the lean-to, for no one could sleep in that cold place ; and un-coffined, it could not be left alone for fear vermin might get near to it.   Therefore thus they had decided.

Tom was busy getting ready the mid-day meal—so much later to-day ; and after dinner Dr. Seagrim was to be accompanied back to the Mission by Charley Kirwan, who was going to buy a coffin* for his brother.   He was to return the next morning.

"I anticipate a frightful storm to-night, Charley," observed the Doctor, "we had better start immediately or we shall be losing our way in the snow."

---

* In the States, coffins of all sizes are kept in stock at the undertaker's.

And soon after the hasty dinner, they started, leaving Tom and Woodhouse alone in the Ranche. Hecker and Lieboldt were out seeing to the cattle.

Tom had tidied the Ranche, washed the dinner things, put on the kettle for tea, heaped high the wood upon the hearth, and gathered a great heap of logs into one corner of the room, enough for the next forty-eight hours.

"We must have some symbol of Christianity near the dead," thought Woodhouse, and so they made a rough wooden cross, placed it upon a tub, and burnt a lamp near it. They forgot the howl of the wind in their occupation. Suddenly Tom jerked out :—

"Why, look at the snow coming in under the door."

They both hurried to the window, and looking out, saw nothing but one great whirl of snow. The air was thick with it ; and they, fascinated, watched the wild storm, as

> "Ever deeper—deeper—deeper,
> Fell the snow o'er all the landscape,
> Fell the covering snow and drifted.'

"Charley won't come to-morrow in that storm."

"Don't say so, Tom."

"You mark my word ; as sure as I'm called Tom, he can't come. There'll be snow so deep, as perhaps us 'll have to dig our way out of the house."

"Tom !"

But Tom was right. There was such a storm that night as few settlers on that prairie remembered.

CHAPTER XIV.

All the land with snow is covered;
All the leaves from all the branches
Fall and fade—and die and wither."—*Longfellow.*

SNOWED UP.

ITH their faces pressed against the window watching the drifting snow, whistling, eddying, driven by the shrieking east wind against the panes, the two inhabitants of the Ranche saw day-light fade, and night grow upon them. The room was full of light from the wood fire and the lamp; and Hecker and Lieboldt coming in half frozen, and looking like snow-men, recalled them to the present. Shaking the snow from them, and crouching near to the fire, the Ranche-men waited for Tom to arrange their tea-table for them. They spoke in whispers—as yet unused to that white-robed object lying yonder on the bed. Hecker glanced round and crossed himself as the wind, sweeping under the door and round by the bed, shook the sheet placed over the dead man's body, and passed in little waves underneath it.

"What an awful night, Mr. Woodhouse; the snow nigh blinded us coming up from the crick."

"It am a fearfool night. If us wish to keep the life in him we must stay by the fire all night. To go to sleep means to be freeze to death."

"Nonsense."

"Nonsense you say. Who sleep in de lean-to?— he be freeze in less than two hour. Who sleep near de roof?—he be freeze too. No, no mein, sir, dat's no nonsense. You not sleep—you lib. You go sleep dere, you die. You keep near de fire, dat be the best place."

And so the whole group huddled round the fire. Meanwhile the wind seemed to grow more strong, more boisterous outside, and successions of gusts coming in through the cracks, and under the doors, absolutely caused the sheet over the dead man's body to shake again and again, as it rippled in wavelets beneath.

"Whist," said the Irishman, "is Doc really dead?"

"Yes;" said Woodhouse, passing over to the bed, and lifting up the sheet from the face of the corpse; and as they looked upon those still set features, illuminated with that same kind smile he had in life, they felt there could be nothing there to be afraid of; and although they must be companions to a corpse throughout the long hours of the night, God the Father of the living and the dead was their father. "Dominus regit me, nihil mihi deerit."

"Sharley won't come to-morrow, nor the next day; the drift will be terrible. I have known the drifts to be thirty feet deep before this."

The new comers to the prairie shuddered. In the meanwhile, Tom had got tea or supper ready; and the warm coffee revived the spirits of the men, who, with rugs and blankets, set about barricading, in a space near the fire, inaccessible, as far as possible, to the constant draughts. And well was it they did so; for many on the lone prairies were frozen to death, in their beds, that terrible night.

And this was the Christmas Eve. To-morrow would be the birthday of the Lord, which was to be kept by these men—snowed up, with a corpse.

A strange Christmas for Willie Woodhouse, who, had Kirwan been by, would have had some one to talk with—some one to console. But with these rough Ranche-men, what could he do?

The Christmas morning broke once again upon the world. Slowly did the grey light gleam upon the prairie world, white with the driven snow; and now the men with spades dug a path out into the day, and down to the creek, and hurried after their cattle, who were sheltered under the trees in places built for them; they had to be fed, although Brown Kirwan lay stiff and cold in the Ranche, on the snow-white prairie. The storm began again after a few hours' respite, and then came the knowledge that no one would venture from the Mission with a coffin that day; and also that none of them could assist at any Offices, at the Mission Church, on Christmas Day.

Tom had been unwell, so he was about the Ranche

in the morning, and with energy was trying to learn some Catechism when his work was done.

"Seven Gods, and three Sacraments."

"Eh? No Tom, no. 'Three persons in God, and seven Sacraments;'" and in this style the wall of Tom's ignorance was being broken down.

And then came the preparation for the Christmas dinner. Roast quail, pork, and chicken; gently, reverently, and with whispered conversation were the preparations made. None forgot that silent white-robed figure, and the rough wooden cross, with the light burning before it. True, there were no bright flowers to make wreaths to lay near the dead; but they had collected some slight branches of a tree, with long thorns two inches in length, and with these they had plaited a crown of thorns—a wreath if you will, and it lay upon the breast of the corpse, the dark shade contrasting strangely against the whiteness of the linen sheet.

Almost in silence was the dinner eaten, and then again began the watch, barricaded near the fire. And so the Christmas Day died upon the Prairies.

CHAPTER XV.

"Out of the bosom of the Air,
    Out of the cloud folds of her garments shaken,
Over the woodlands brown and bare,
    Over the harvest-fields forsaken,
        Silent, and soft, and slow
        Descends the snow."

—

"Even as our cloudy fancies take
    Suddenly shape in some divine expression,
Even as the troubled heart doth make,
    In the white countenance confession,
        The troubled sky reveals
        The grief it feels."

Longfellow.

THE SNOW-CLAD CEMETERY.—THE STATION.

BROWN KIRWAN lay in his coffin; Charley had brought the coffin upon an ox waggon to the Ranche the day before this chapter opens. He was to be buried in one of the Northern States, whither all the Kirwans were taken. The brother Charley Kirwan loved so much was to be disinterred, and the two coffins were to be taken by train those hundreds of miles to the Northern State by Charley Kirwan himself, who was to start from the

Mission in two days. Woodhouse was to stay at the Ranche during his absence. All this had been arranged, and men engaged to open the grave in the Prairie Cemetery.

"Poor Charley; you have grown very white, and old-looking these days."

"I feel so, Willie; I feel aged more than I can tell you. I dread dis-interring that body to-morrow, and I have to face my mother with the coffined remains of the two sons she loved most of us all."

"I can help you to-morrow, Charley; I will superintend at the Cemetery for you."

"Oh, thank you so much, then I can go on to the Mission, and make my arrangements at the Railway Station concerning their removal—(pointing in the direction of the iron case)—and the other coffin, when it arrives at the Mission, must be packed in acids and ice in an outer case; meanwhile I must send supplies up here to last until my return."

"Oh, Charley, how I shall miss you!" and for the first time in all that sadness and trouble his calmness deserted him.

"Don't you remember our text? 'Mine eyes are ever toward the Lord; for He shall pluck my feet out of the net.' As long as we don't look aside from Him, He will pluck our feet out of the net of trouble and of absence; and whilst I go my sad journey, you will have one equally as sad, riding from Ranche to Ranche amongst sickness and death here."

"I had forgotten that, Charley."

"I have not forgotten it ; and I know your reward : 'Inasmuch as ye did it unto one of the least of these my brethren, ye did it unto Me.'"

"*Unto Him.* Well, how consoling it is, to think that we can bank some of our good actions in the Bank of God's charity."

"That is what Brown did. Poor Brown, God rest his soul."

*   *   *   *   *

It is the early morning on the Prairies. An ox waggon stands at Kirwan's Ranche. With muffled steps and slow, men carry their sad burden from the Ranche door and place it upon the waggon. A large crimson and black, square pattern, travelling shawl is thrown pall-wise across the coffin, and on it rests a crown of thorns. How bright the crimson shows up against the white back-ground of snow—snow, snow everywhere. The men stand bare-headed in the intensely cold air ; and Tom, with tears in his eyes, murmurs "Good-bye, Doc. ; poor Doc."

Woodhouse, clad in a long coat and snow-shoes, and muffled in furs, comes out and gets into the waggon near the coffin. Meanwhile another waggon, drawn by oxen, advances ; four men are riding in it—and start first on their way to the Prairie Cemetery, followed slowly by the second waggon. And thus began Brown Kirwan's funeral procession.

*   *   *   *   *

Two waggons stand on the snow-whitened Prairie, waiting on a rising ground near to a railed-in enclosure, whilst, with pick-axe and spade, four men are busily employed opening a grave, closed not so very long ago. One waggon, with sleek white oxen attached to it, and covered with a crimson and black, pall-like envelopement, we recognise as that which stood at Kirwan's Ranche not long since. A muffled, dark figure stands near, and his head is bowed over the coffin upon the crimson covering.

What a picture for an Artist !—that great stretch of Prairie with the dim sky overhead, and the only thing near (speaking of animation) being those four men, throwing up the dark mould upon the pure snow, carrying on in grim silence their gloomy work. How bitterly cold it was the actions showed, as they stopped every now and again to rub the exposed parts of their bodies with snow.

What a cruel day. What a sad task.

But now from the gloomy bowels of the earth is heaved up that clayey mass of substance mother earth had claimed. Shut within the mortuary casket, it is dragged to the surface, and reverently placed upon the empty waggon ; earth clinging to the coffin lid as its only pall. But no :

> " Silent, and soft, and slow
> Descends the snow,"

making the earth-bedrabbled coffin-lid pure and clean as the Prairie men hoped his spirit then was.

And once more over that silent Prairie the doubly sad procession winds towards the Mission. At a great distance in front was the coffin just taken from the ground.

The worst was over now, there was only the cold and piercing wind to bear; and that must be borne, for walking in the snow was impossible, although the road taken was a higher one, from which the snow of some days past had been blown away by the high wind, so that it was just possible for waggons to travel along. And nearing the Mission, curious Ranchers peered from their doors to see anything so unusual pass. Some would say, " Poor Doc Kirwan "; others would murmur a prayer, or cross themselves; and towards the evening, frozen almost to stupidity, the assistants and drivers of the waggons arrived at the Station near the Mission.

A group of people stood on the rough wooden platform, amongst them Charley Kirwan. One coffin was to be "anchored on the prairie" in the waggon until the outer casket could come, and the chemicals and ice were brought down to pack it in. Doc. Kirwan's friends at the Mission carried his body into the left luggage office, where it was to remain until the morning.

A gentleman Rancher at the Station, seeing the exhausted condition of Woodhouse, prevailed on him to accept some of the contents of his flask, and invited him to visit him at his Ranche, near Walnut Creek.

"I am a Methodist," he said at parting, "but I can appreciate the true Catholicity of your conduct to-day. You will visit me, won't you, at my Ranche?"

"If I can be of any use to you I will come."

"If I can be of any use," quoted the stranger; "and if I send to you, being seized by the epidemic, will you come to me?"

"I will."

"At day or night?"

"At day or night."

He was smiling, yet with tears in his eyes, as he bade his new friend Good-bye; and Mr. MacAntham said at parting, "It is a bargain you come, and I shall call you 'little Priest.'"

"Why? I am not that."

"No, but you have a truly apostolic soul—keep it always Christ-like."

CHAPTER XVI.

"Complain not that the way be long—what Road is weary
    that leads there?
But let the Angel take thine hand and lead thee up the
    misty stair,
And then with beating heart await, the opening of the
    golden gate."

Proctor.

THE DEACON'S BOY.

DEACON WRANTON sat by his fireside; his head bowed upon his hands, and a great sorrow pressing upon his heart. The heart of Deacon Wranton was breaking, and thus in anguish and silence, disturbed only by his ejaculatory prayers, did he tell out his suffering to God. The Deacon's Ranche was hard by the Cemetery, from which in the morning the body of Henry Kirwan had been removed; in fact, the Cemetery touched upon the extremity of the Deacon's farm.

Deacon Wranton had been a successful settler (one of the few), who had gathered together a nice home and surroundings about him. His wife was bright and thrifty, also his eldest son Albert the pride of the neighbouring Ranches for his innate cleverness, gentility, and handsome looks. Perhaps in his heart of hearts the Deacon worshipped this bright youth, growing up to manhood under his eyes; and hearing his praises for goodness, kindliness and gentleness sung on all sides by his neighbours he might be surely pardoned.

The Deacon's heart was breaking because the fell epidemic was there—*there*, in his house. The comeliest of all his children lay low on the bed of illness, and the Doctor pronounced it spino-meningitis.

At the first Penny Reading on the Prairies a meeting was organised for nursing the sick: it was started for the young men of the neighbourhood by Woodhouse, who himself was at the head of it. Indefatigably had Albert laboured to keep the energy of his comrades un-impaired in this good work, whilst he himself stayed up with the sick two nights a week. Albert and Woodhouse were to be seen everywhere amongst the sick, and near them, following on their footsteps in the work was Miss Dempsey, exerting all that gentle earnestness of hers to keep the women up to their standard of day-nursing.

"Oh, my son, my son," murmured the Deacon, "my son, my son; would God that I could die for thee," and in the flickering fire-light one saw great bead-like drops raining from his eyes—falling diamond-like between the fingers of the hand covering his face.

"Deacon, Deacon, some more cabbages are wanted," called his wife from the other room.

"I will go, I will go."

And out into the cold started the Deacon to fetch the cabbages from the out-house.

"Deacon, Deacon, place these on his back, we want some help," were the words the Deacon was saluted with on re-entering the Ranche.

"All right, my wife; this illness is the Lord's doing, and is marvellous in our eyes."

The Deacon tried to speak cheerily, but his voice was tear-stained; it trembled, it quavered, it touched such a chord in that wife's heart, that she leant her head against that broad shoulder, and her smothered heart-sobs found vent in tears.

"Hush, he will hear; he is not asleep."

"Oh, my boy, my beautiful boy to go down to his grave so."

Taking her two hands, clasping them in his, and looking deep down into those tearful eyes and into that sorrowful heart, he whispered, "I can do all things, through Him who comforteth me — who comforteth me in striking my first-loved son—I can do all things, we can do all things, we *can* bear this."

And those two trusting hearts knelt and asked courage of God.

"Father, bring me the leaves now if you can."

"I am coming Albert;" and going to the bed-side in the next room he took off the leaves from the poor

blistered spine, and placed other warm ones there—other
boiled cabbage leaves. When that operation was finished
—and excruciating agony it brought to Albert as each
one was separately removed, and *that* somewhat clumsily
by those untrained attendants—almost fainting the boy
asked his father to let Mr. Woodhouse know of his
illness.

The Deacon's brow was puckered with care, for he
affected not the Mission and a set form of Catholic
Religion. He hardly ever entered the little town excepting for groceries, or other business, either to buy
or sell; but it grieved the Deacon's heart to see the
first establishment for many miles round, that of the
Catholic Faith. With a secret joy the Deacon watched
growing up in the Mission an Episcopal Church (Anglican)
and a Methodist Conventicle. With a peculiar energy he
started each Sunday twice to the prayer meetings held
in the boarded building of the Conventicle upon the
Prairies near to Fort Scott. How fervently he prayed
for the spread of his faith; yet now his son asked for
this stranger to nurse him.

During this while the boy's dark brown eyes were
fixed upon his father's face.

"Why do you wish this Albert? Do you want him
to come and see you?"

"I wish him to know; he may be nursing others,
but he will come to me in my turn, he promised me
should I be ill to do so."

The Deacon sighed a great sigh, and bowed his head;

and then Miss Dempsey entering, Albert asked her to let Mr. Woodhouse know.

"I will do so, Albert, to-morrow; to-day he is at the Mission. I saw him go with Doc Kirwan's coffin."

"And soon he will stand by Albert Wranton's," replied the boy.

"Oh, Albert, don't mistrust God in this way."

"I don't mistrust Him, Miss Dempsey, but I feel I must pack up my trunks for a long journey from this world to the next."

"Are you frightened to go that journey?"

"I don't think so. I have thought a great deal whilst I was nursing the sick in their rough homes these last nights. I have asked God to forgive me all my faults. I feel in this illness as I did those dark nights on the prairies. I am walking or riding home through the darkness to God my Father. Tired out as I was I always was glad to get back to father and home. Pained out as I am now, with little chance of recuperating, I shall be glad to go home to 'My Lord, and my God;'" and then he moaned, "My Lord and my God," and a minute after was delirious, speaking of his turkeys, and wandering away to the woodlands adjoining the creek, where he had been catching cardinal birds only the other day.

"Poor Bertie," softly came from the lips of Miss Dempsey, as she laid her cool hand on the boy's burning brow.

The Deacon and his wife were kneeling round that

sick bed praying: "Aye, great is thy faith; if God wills, be it done unto thee according to thy word."

*   *   *   *

Some evenings later, in the bright moonlight, over the snowy Prairie rode a muffled figure towards the Ranche of Wranton. Arrived there he sought an empty place in the stable, and attended to his horse, feeding it and taking off the saddle, and then he walked to the little wooden piazza outside the kitchen. Knocking at the door, no voice bade him enter: but entering he saw a figure near the fire plunged deep in reverie. It was Deacon Wranton.

"Good evening, Deacon."

"Aye; the Lord be with thee. Who art thou?"

"A friend of Albert's."

"Ah," coldly observed the Deacon, "his Mission friend, of whom he is always talking in his wanderings. Come though, and see if you can do anything to nurse our invalid."

Taking off his coat and wraps he followed the Deacon to the adjoining room.

There lay Albert Wranton, that always spiritual face of his, more spiritual now, as the disease had touched it with a look so refined, so Ghirlandaijo-like that one could imagine it a figure stepped into life from the canvas of that great master.

Scarcely eighteen winters had swept their snow over his snowy brow, and now in his gentleness and purity the Great Sweet Voice was calling to him—"Come up higher." He lay with the light shining on his face, and that usual complement of illness, the friends of the family gazing at him.

He was wandering now in that semi-conscious state, sure token of long illness. He was quoting something he had heard from the Indians. "I heard the voice of the Great Spirit in the cry of the Red-bird. I sought him in the rustling of the leaves upon the trees. I found him in the laughing of the waters. I searched for him in man." And then came a pause, "Ah, my turkeys. I know them—two, four, six, eight, twenty. I know my turkeys. I shall sell them. Yes, I think so." And then, "I wonder if Mr. Woodhouse will come, or Charley Kirwan?"

The new-comer made his way softly to the bed-side, and laid his hand in Albert's. "Albert, do you know me?"

With a bright conscious look he woke up: "Oh, Mr. Woodhouse, yes; I am so glad you have come— don't leave me now."

And so he was installed nurse off and on at the Deacon's.

*   *   *   *

After seventy-five days!

Woodhouse had stayed a day or so at the Wrantons', as often as he was able to leave the other sick people in the district. Albert always wished for Baptism, but the Deacon disapproved of his receiving this Sacrament, and would never allow any of the Nursing Association to have water near them, for fear his son should be baptized unbeknown to him.

Albert was near his end, and on this day begged so hard for them to open to him the Gates of Life, that Woodhouse complied. Albert said a Squaw brought her baby five hundred miles for Baptism, and God says— 'Except ye be baptized of water and the Holy Ghost, ye cannot enter into the Kingdom of Heaven.' "I want to enter; do baptize me. God will not call me until you do, and I want to go." One of those standing by brought some water in a large silver spoon, and in a few moments Albert was numbered with the great army of the baptized, and according to the teaching of the Catholic Church, as the water fell upon his brow and the solemn words were uttered, his original, venial and mortal sins were washed away.

On the eightieth day Albert died. His kind actions and pure life were as a light in a dark night to many, leading them to better things.

Deacon Wranton's joy in life passed away with the spirit of his boy, who from the great Indian legends and practical Indian fidelity to Christianity had himself learnt more of that Highest Good, that "Summum Bonum," GOD, than he had learned from the whites.

Miss Dempsey wrote the news to Woodhouse in these words :—"Schools are out, and I stopped a few moments to write this. Orange Wranton just came to tell me that '*Albert is dead!*' Poor boy, poor boy! God grant him happiness—he suffered so much. I hope his sufferings are over. Death is so terrible. This going out into the darkness with only hope. And yet let us try ever so hard, we 'know not whether we meet love or hatred' on the other shore. It is no wonder so many poor creatures despair."

CHAPTER XVII.

AT THE MISSION HOUSE.—DEATHS FROM FREEZING.

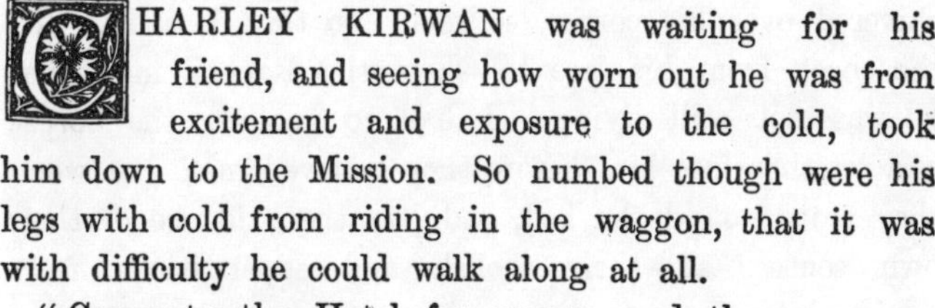

CHARLEY KIRWAN was waiting for his friend, and seeing how worn out he was from excitement and exposure to the cold, took him down to the Mission. So numbed though were his legs with cold from riding in the waggon, that it was with difficulty he could walk along at all.

"Come to the Hotel for supper, and then we can go on to the Mission."

But they met the old Superior looking for them; his kind heart told him they were worn out with fatigue, and the quiet of the Mission House would be more akin to them than the noisy Hotel in the little town. And then he informed them of the numerous deaths from freezing. Two young Ranchers on the Creek were found frozen dead in their beds. A waggon was discovered on

the borders of Missouri and Kansas with thirteen people
"on board" lying under a tarpaulin dead. The driver
frozen also, and, when discovered, holding in his hands
the reins of his frozen team. And it was not only
in one quarter, but reports of like accidents were coming
in to the Mission from every quarter.

"And how did you escape?"

"We stayed up all night: made enormous fires, and
barricaded ourselves against draughts with blankets and
rugs."

"Well done, well done! You begin to know something of our prairie life now."

"But it was terrible during the storm. The wind
blew under the sheet covering poor Brown's body and
shivered over his corpse, so much so that I had to lift
the sheet from his face to show the Ranche men that
he was not still living. I had to uncover the corpse
and let them see him before they believed me; but when
they stood round the bed, and had the evidence of their
own senses, all their foolish and superstitious fears
vanished."

"Were you frightened of your Christmas Eve?"

"No; but it would have been pleasanter for me with
Charley to talk to, but of course one can't regret doing
one's duty."

"Well, it is the time of 'the Haustus,'* come to the
Refectory, and have some warm coffee, or something

---

* "Haustus," a slight refreshment served at four o'clock (consisting
in this case of coffee and bread) in the Houses of "the Society."

more substantial if you wish; and for you my young friend, I recommend warmth and sleep after your refreshment."

Although in these days of non-hero worship, when the height of refinement externally is to regard everything with the complacence of a tame tortoise, whatever one may feel or think internally, yet one cannot help admiring that rugged old Superior who had given the best days of his life to a cause he believed so thoroughly in. He was one amongst men, who in those dark days that befell his country, had saved his crown of spiritual manhood; escaping from black materialism, and revolutionary deluges, with God, freedom of conscience, and immortality of nobleness still his. A king amongst men. A man who claimed no country now but that "Fatherland above." A man who refused himself even the pleasure of speaking the language of his own country out of self-denial, and spoke only the language of his adopted country, and his dear Indians. All honour be to men of this stamp, for they are scattered few and far between in the furrows of life.

"You leave to-morrow, Charley, I presume?"

"Yes, by an early train, I start with the two coffins. Woodhouse goes with me to the creek, the train stops there, and he will go back to the Ranche and his sick people."

"I almost wonder he did not go with you."

"He preferred remaining behind until the epidemic ceases. I shall find him here on my return; and you know my theory, that a dose of Prairie life improves all Europeans. I for one think he will be better for the sadness, misery and death he has been amongst here."

"I don't gainsay it, Charley, but I will look after him during your absence. I don't think he will be lonely; he gets on with the Prairie people very well."

* * * *

In the early morning, in the train the two friends separated, one to plod over the waste of snow to the Ranche, the other to face a father and mother with his sad burden.

Yet it is only one page in the great history of humanity.

Wearied almost to death, and nearly losing himself in the cross country journey to Kirwan's Ranche, walking sometimes for twenty feet or so up to his knees in snow on the skirt of the great drifts, Woodhouse at last arrived at the Ranche. Tom had been out winter fishing on the creek, and a plentiful supply of fish awaited them for dinner.

In the course of the afternoon a strange pain struck Woodhouse in the chest; thinking it only cold, or some little inflammation, he put on a mustard plaster, and lay down on the bed, and fell into a deep dreamless sleep, until Tom awoke him for supper. Supper without Charley Kirwan seemed dull and listless. Everybody was too tired out to clear away the *debris*, the men were half dozing over their pipes, when an unusual occurrence at the Ranche—a knock sounded at the door.

Tom opened it. A young fellow whose coat was

covered with snow entered, asking if it was Kirwan's Ranche.

"Yes, my friend; what do you want? Charley Kirwan's gone North to bury his two brothers; went by train to-day. Yer can't see him."

"I don't want him. I want his guest. I come from Mr. MacAntham's; he has the epidemic very badly, and is dying, and he raves for Mr. Woodhouse to go and nurse him."

"Then he shan't go," says Tom.

"He *must go*," observed the stranger. "He gave his word to MacAntham at the station. MacAntham asked him, 'If I send to you, being taken by the epidemic, will you come to me?' And then he says, 'I will.' MacAntham says, 'By day or night.' Then he replied, 'By day or by night.' It's night now, sure enough, and a snowy night too, and I've come for him."

"Then," replies Tom, "He shan't go; he can't ride; he ain't well; he can't walk that distance."

"No, nor I over the Prairie, but if we make for the line, we can walk along that, the snow is less deep there."

"He shan't go," says Tom again, "he shan't go. He's ourn now, and we won't let him out."

"Wall, I guess MacAntham's dying, and the Minister's there and a crowd of folks praying; but MacAntham raves only for Mr. Woodhouse," and looking towards him the stranger says, "You'll come, eh friend?"

"Yes, I'll come," but it was a shuddering sound, a

dread of that long snowy walk — a "Yes, I'll come," tired by recent excitement and death.

"You can't ride, snow's too deep, you must go as I go."

"Tom, give him something to eat, he has walked nigh six miles."

"I can't wait to eat now, friend; when we get there will do."

And so equipped in Tom's long knee boots, which he insisted on Woodhouse wearing, and wrapped in a long coat and scarf, out into the snowy night passed the two strangers to each other, to toil once again over that tiring snow, through the long hours until they reached MacAntham's Ranche.

CHAPTER XVIII.

"Kind hearts are here; yet would the tenderest one
Have limits to its mercy: God has none.
And man's forgiveness may be true and sweet,
But yet he stoops to give it. More complete
Is love that lays forgiveness at thy feet,
And pleads with thee to raise it. Only Heaven
Means *crowned*, not *vanquished*, when it says
Forgiven."—*Proctor.*

THE FREEMASON'S DEATH AND BURIAL.

GIVE me your hand, mister. I'm Tom Sheehy, one on 'em whose adopted the nursing our sick Ranchers at nights. Albert Wranton taught me what you said about it, how by nursing them we was nursing Christ; and he sez, as how you sez, that's what that text means, 'Inasmuch as ye did it to one of the least of these my Brethren ye did it unto Me.' Well, I didn't walk all this way for MacAntham particularly; I walked here for Christ, cos if he was on earth I'm sure I shouldn't stop to hum (at home) if he sent me on a message."

"Yes, Christ indeed says, 'I was sick and ye visited me.' That must console us, Tom Sheehy, for our long tiring walk over the snow to-night : if we think every step we take is a step for Christ—and certainly we want some hope to guide us over this snowy waste."

"Now don't you fear, mister. I know every foot of the Prairie round here. I must own it's really dreadful for a stranger—the darkness, and the deep snow, and these flakes that fall every now and again. It's lonesome like to strangers, this great silence on the broad prairie, but then, as poor Albert used to say, 'It's for Christ.'"

"Did you know Albert long ?"

"Yes, we were great friends, Albert and me. He was one of those who could snare a red-bird with any one, or hunt the fish well too, and Albert, after all, was somewhat of a scholard."

"So Miss Dempsey said."

There was silence now for a little while between the travellers. Tom was peering into the darkness, but his strong hand grasped the one in his, to give his companion confidence.

"Are we far off MacAntham's Ranche, Tom ?"

"We ain't near it yet. The wind blows cold though, don't it ? and the snow's deep here. A fierce night for the spirit to go out of the body, eh ? Oh, mister, *I am* sorry MacAntham's dying."

"How long has he been ill ?"

"I dunnow. They was all struck about the same time like — first his wife and grandchild, then him, and now they all lies sick together, the little grandchild in one room, MacAntham in another, and the wife upstairs. Shure it would be dreadful expenses for him, only his son-in-law is a doctor. Them MacAnthams' rich people like for the Prairies—and Mr. MacAntham's head of them Freemasons round here. I heerd tell as if he died there 'ud be grand doings, for all them Masons for a hundred miles round would be coming out to bury him. There now, never you mind that snow—shure, but it drifts a bit in your eyes, and the sleepers be slippery like; but we're agoin' to 'tend Christ, mister; don't you see MacAntham—see Christ, and the way won't be a dreary."

"How far are we from the Ranche now, Tom?"

"A mile and a half, may be; bear up, Mister, the way's roughish, but every step yer takes counts in God's book, 'cos its for His sick."

How Woodhouse crawled over that last mile and a half he never knew; the cowman's hard boots he walked in, wet through as they were, chafed his feet at every step, until the agony became almost unendurable; the snow drifting into his eyes, and the intense cold, seemed little in comparison to this.

"There, now; there!" cried Tom joyfully, "there is the light in his kitchen, we'll soon be up to it, and I told them to get dry stockings for you, and summat to eat; and a good fire will prepare you for that sad work you've got to do—get a man's soul ready to see God. Oh, me; Oh, me; it's little time you've got to do your work in: he'll die by the morning light."

"Why did he send for me, Tom Sheehy? Why didn't he send for one of the Priests from the Mission?"

"Why, 'cos he said as how he was struck with a young 'un like you a taking down of Doc. Kirwan's coffin to the Mission."

"Well, that's a very simple procedure."

"He didn't think so; he sez you as come for enjoying yourself a spending nights with they sick; you as come out a gentleman, a waiting about that freezing day in the Cemetery, 'that's the man for me,' sez he, 'he'll tell me something more about God than I know.'"

"Tom Sheehy, he was looking to the man instead of to Christ. The Holy Ghost only can infuse love into his nature; the Holy Ghost only can teach him how to enter into the fold of the Church."

"I 'spose yer right, but it's strange these men a sending off for you when they're a dying. Will he get in the Church?"

"I believe so, for wherever the love of God is, is Jesus Christ; wherever Jesus Christ is, the Church is with Him; *and if it is true that every Christian is obliged to unite himself to the body of the Church as soon as he knows of Her existence*, it is certain also that *invincible ignorance* withdraws him from this law, leaving him under the immediate government of Jesus Christ, the first and sovereign Father of all Christianity."

"Then, there's hope for MacAntham?"

"Hope! yes, Tom Sheehy, no human eye can embrace the extent of Holy Church, and those who would place certain barriers, which in their eyes appear valid, have no idea of that double radiation of Her nature."

"God be thanked. Through this wicket now, Sir, and we are at the door."

* * * * *

Out from the cold, the deep snow, the silence and the wintry night, into the warm kitchen, and the kind though hushed welcome.

Miss MacAntham and her two brothers were waiting in the doorway, as soon as they heard the gate clicking. "The sick man was so anxious," they said, "about the long walk he had given Mr. Woodhouse." Warm woollen stockings were airing at the fire, and hot coffee and supper waiting for them. He would rather go to Mr. MacAntham at once.

"No," replied the Doctor, "he will live until the morning, and I can't have you ill here, which you certainly will be, unless you take something to keep you up after the fatigue of a long snowy walk."

Getting rid of those hard boots, enjoying a footbath and putting on warm thick stockings in the Ranche kitchen was short work, but luxury itself after that long walk over the Prairies.

The young Doctor, the son-in-law of MacAntham, was a fine-built fellow, with fair complexion, regular features, and light hair; his clothes were in the last New York fashion, and he had with him a gentle winning way. He was but eight-and-twenty, he had recently lost his wife, and his little daughter was very near death's door in the house; also her grandmother and grandfather-in-law. He (the Doctor) had but lately left New York to make a practice for himself out West, and he arrived at home in time to attend upon his own parents, who were both at death's door. He was a Catholic, and one of the Fathers from the Mission had but yesterday baptized his little girl. Of the other people in the house, there were two sisters, two brothers, and the father and mother.

This much the Doctor told Woodhouse as he sat by him, whilst he partook hastily of some refreshment, and then telling him of the illness of his father-in-law, he added, "It must end fatally; I can see no hope myself, and I am distressed beyond measure, as I am afraid of the shock to the system of my mother his death will cause. I wanted to have him make his peace with God yesterday, when the Father was here, but he refused. Now, I will take you to him, and then I must go back to the bed-side of my mother." Thus saying, he opened a door leading from the kitchen to a sitting-room. Congregated together in this room were six or seven men and women, friends of the sick persons, sitting around the French stove which stood far out into the room; these, as usual, had gathered there directly the first news of the sickness reached them. Amongst them was a Dissenting Minister, a man about forty, who, directly he perceived two Catholics passing through the room, opened a very large family Bible, and read aloud, in a stentorian voice, chapter after chapter. In bed, in one corner of the room, lay Rosie Lister, a sweet child of seven years, with long, streaming, golden curls of the colour of her father's hair, falling around her dear little face. They talked for a few minutes with her, and then opening a door off one side of the room they entered the sick man's bedroom. There lay Mr. MacAntham in the simply furnished room, his white face and long shaggy locks contrasting strangely with the snowy linen around him. His breathing was oppressed, but a glad light shone in his eyes as they fell upon his young friend, whom he had only seen once before at the Osage Station, under such peculiar circumstances.

The Doctor leant over the dying man, listened to his breathing, felt his pulse, examined his tongue, gave him a spoonful of some jelly-like substance, and then, as he finished the examination, led Woodhouse to the next room and whispered in his ear, "The congestion has passed, he will die in the early morning ; what you have to say to him, say quickly. I must go and prepare my mother for the end." Returning to the room, sitting there in the shaded light he recognised Miss Dempsey. As she left the room, she motioned to him and whispered, "If you want anything, or he requires any nursing, I shall be in the next room."

And then he was alone with the dying man.

"I am dying, sir," MacAntham gasped, "dying ! I feel it, I know it, and I want you to explain to me all the belief of the Catholic Church." He put out his hand and grasped that of Woodhouse. " I made you promise if I was seized with the epidemic that you would come to me, and I see you have kept your word: 'At day or night.' Oh, I remember it so well,—the Station, the one offensive smelling coffin anchored for the time on the Prairie, and the body of Doctor Kirwan we carried so solemnly into the left luggage office at the Station. But now the hours are short, teach me the religion that made you go through this."

And thus in the dim midnight, amidst the gaspings of that dying man, the great and solemn truths of the Catholic Faith were explained, and consoled one more heart panting after that truth, ever ancient, ever new. And in the stillness both teacher and taught felt that in their midst stood *One* who nearly nineteen hundred years ago promised to send the Comforter into the world to guide it into all truth.

And the Comforter was there that night, and a solemn awe fell upon their souls.

" Miss Dempsey,"—he had to call twice, or thrice, for the good Minister was reading and praying aloud in that stentorian voice of his—" Miss Dempsey, will you bring me some pure water in a basin, and a witness also ? "

A few minutes elapsed and she brought some pure water into the sick room, and with her came Mr. Clay from a Ranche hard by, who was waiting in the sitting room to do what he could for his friend. As they entered, they heard the sick man gasping, " And must I resign all secret societies, even the Freemasons."

"I am sorry to say Yes, for I think that grieves you; but the Catholic Church forbids her children belonging to any secret Society whatsoever."

"Then I resign them all, for I must be baptized of water and the Holy Ghost; I only desire to obey my God and enter into the kingdom he has promised."

And then those simple words broke the silence of the sick room as the baptismal stream flowed over another brow. "John, I baptize thee, in the Name of the Father, and of the Son, and of the Holy Ghost. Amen."

And a gladder light grew in MacAntham's eyes, and a more peaceful look spread over the wan face. He pressed the hand still wet with the baptismal water, and whispered, "Joy in the presence of God over one sinner doing penance."

The Doctor came to see if Mrs. MacAntham could come and visit his father, to bid her last earthly farewell. Ill as she was, she could not bear the thought of parting from her husband, or that he should die without her being by to nurse that dear head. Just risen from her sick bed, muffled up in wrappers, and supported by her son and her two daughters, she came and stood by that dying bed. The grey light of the early dawn was vainly struggling to penetrate the inky darkness. There was no violent disturbed grief, but that silence deeper than words, and great tears falling from the wife's eyes, "Hast thou found Him, husband. Is He precious?"

"Doubly so until the day break, and the shadows flee away."

And then husband and wife were left alone to bid their last farewell. Later they were all standing in the sick room, the family and the guests, and the Minister was praying softly, for he saw the soul was about to break away from the captivity of the body. The eyes of the dying man wandered over those loved faces he was leaving, and a great light of love and thankfulness beamed from those eyes, as they lit for a moment upon the Minister's face, who in a soft tenor sang with exquisite pathos :

> " The city paved with gold,
>   Bright with each dazzling gem,
>   Swift shall thine eyes behold
>   The new Jerusalem.
>   Yea lo ! e'en now in viewless might,
>   Uprise the walls of living light."

But John MacAntham heard not the last words : he was within the city. The earthly morning had dawned for those around his death-bed ; but a newer and gladder day had broken for him, never to be followed by night, or darkened by earthly sorrow.

*   *   *   *

Some hours later the Doctor and Woodhouse were talking in the sitting-room, preparatory to his returning to Kirwan's Ranche.

" Is he to be buried according to the Rites of the Catholic Church ? "

" I don't think I should urge that, Doctor ; what does it harm his soul ? freshly baptized, and joying in God. Let them bury him as they will."

" I suppose the Minister will perform the Rite—it is my mother's wish."

"And it might do her harm to gainsay it."

"I am so glad you agree with me in this."

Three days after, nearly one hundred Freemasons followed the Master of their Lodge to his burial upon the vast Prairie, in a new Cemetery, several miles distant from where young Kirwan had been buried. The Master of the Lodge, after prayer, deposited in the grave the lambskin or white apron, the emblem of innocence and the badge of a Mason, and then the Brethren moving in procession round the grave, severally dropped into it a sprig of evergreen, typical of Immortality, after which public grand honours were given. Both arms were crossed on the breast, the left uppermost, and the open palms of the hands striking the shoulders ; they were then raised above the head, the palms striking each other, and made to fall sharply on the thighs with the head bowed. This was repeated three times. Whilst the honours were being given the third time, the Brethren audibly pronounced the following words, when the arms were crossed on the breast, "We cherish his memory here ;" when the hands were extended over the head, "We commend his spirit to God who gave it ;" and when the hands were extended towards the ground, "And consign his body to the earth." The Master conducting the Office finished in these words, "Let us improve this solemn warning, that at last when the sheeted dead are stirring, when the great white throne is set, we shall receive from the Omniscient Judge the thrilling invitation,

'Come ye blessed, inherit the kingdom prepared for you from the foundation of the World.'" Then followed a hymn, the last verse of which ran thus:

"Thou art gone to the grave; but t'were wrong to deplore thee,
When God was thy trust, and thy guardian and guide;
He gave thee, He took thee, and soon will restore thee
In the blest Lodge above where the faithful abide."

Then followed a prayer, to which all responded—"So mote it be."

CHAPTER XIX.

"I see, but cannot reach, the height,
  That lies for ever in the light;
  And yet for ever and for ever,
  When seeming just within my grasp,
  I feel my feeble hands unclasp,
  And sink discouraged into night;
  For thine own purpose, thou hast sent
  The strife, and the discouragement."—*Longfellow.*

TOM AT THE MISSION.

TOM and Woodhouse were thrown together a great deal during this time at the Ranche. Tom taught him all he knew of coons and coon hunting; all he knew about wild animals and their ways; how to swim over the dangerous parts of the creeks on horse back, and the hundred and one ins and outs of Prairie life. All these things were entered into with keen zest. Tom with his Prairie life and thoughts was a great study. One day after cleaning up the Ranche he said, "Now look ye here, I'm going off to school at nine o'clock, and I wants yer to cut my hair." His auditor's eyebrows went high up on to his forehead after the delivery of this strange request. "Now I sits here, there's the scissors" (snibbers Tom called them), "you cuts away, and then them gals and boys won't laugh at me so."

"All right, Tom," and with a broad grin on his face Woodhouse set to work at this hitherto unwonted task.

"I tell yer what," said Tom, when it was done, "I calls yer broke in now. When you comed I said yer weren't broke in; yer had none of our education, yer was ignorant, though Charley said yer knowed a lot about Ropean life" (European, Tom meant), looking up at him with pride Tom thought him an apt pupil. "I teached yer to like it. When I were ill yer teached me some caterchism; now I wants yer to go on with it and to teach me some more; I tries to be good yer knows, and though I never gets it right about the pursons in God, I loves him. I allers sez seven pursons and three Sacraments, or three pursons and seven Sacraments; numbers puzzles me, and yet I loves God's son."

"I've been a good bit away, Tom, but I want to know, do you say your prayers regularly?"

"Not in that loft," said he, pointing with his finger towards the ladder, "not there; sometimes though on a load of hay, with the fresh air and sunshine around me, I tell all in my heart to God. And when I see they cattle moving round, or the corn coming green out of the ground, I sez to myself, 'Tom, some one made 'em.' Charley showed me his watch, I see the springs, the wheels, and the hands, and I sez, 'Who made him?' 'A watchmaker in Geeva' (Geneva), Charley says, so when

I sees all these things—that ere corn, them cattle, myself a movin and growing and springin about—I sez, 'Who made 'em, Tom? Who made 'em?' and then I answers, 'some one.' Well, it's that *some one* I prays to."

"How long is it since you did this, Tom?"

"One summer evening at Groghan's, I see Missis Groghan crush up a beetle with her shoe. I had been a watching of that beetle—the knowingest cunningest way he had of getting food home to his house. Thinks I to myself, man's mighty clever; man can do a' most anything, but he can't make a beetle; all that cunning little life in him man can't put there. Mrs. Groghan crushed that beetle up, but Mr. Groghan couldn't put it together again. Mr. Groghan could do a' most anything, but not that. That set me a thinking, and so I prayed to the Spirit that made the beetle. That may be is God; in fact, since you've teached me, I know it is; and oh, I does love to say that bit o' prayer, 'Our Father.' When I go to the crick for water, or to the carel, or to the Ranche, it's so nice to think—Tom, you never knowed your earthly father, but there over your head, and around you is somebody who cares for Tom. Sometimes when I sees an ant's nest, or a woodpecker walking up a tree, or a fish a swimming in the crick, I begins thinking again about it all; then I sez, 'Tom, yer head can't reach it,' so I ends up with 'Our Father,' and that's a comfort to me. Life seems nicer since you and Charley Kirwan came this way."

"Do you want to learn some more about who made the animals, Tom, something new about God?"

"Oh, yes. So much time every day, half-an-hour in the evenings at cattlechisms" (catechism Tom meant).

"Very well, Tom, we can begin to-night."

Tom, when he came in, found his longtop-boots cleaned and oiled, standing by the fire; a long, dirty task it had been, nevertheless Woodhouse had done it for him, as Tom was busy at his school and with other work. A new life was growing up around Tom; he was getting to know that someone really cared for him. Woodhouse was away visiting some sick person, and Tom being alone in the Ranche sat down and had a good cry by the fire-side. It was such a new sweet idea to him that God was his Father, that all men were his brothers in that blessed brotherhood established by the Son of Mary. And at that moment Tom knew why it was Kirwan and Woodhouse were so anxious to do all they could for the poor, the sick, the dying, and the ignorant. "And 'cos he loves God, and men in God, he cleaned my boots, and dirty work it was too, and him with his nice clothes on a-doing of that. Well, Tom, yer won't shrink from doing what yer don't fancy for the future, will yer? Calls it 'taking up his cross' he does. Well, Tom, you must take up yours;" and from that moment Tom did right willingly.

Hecker coming in disturbed his soliloquy, as Hecker, tired out and hungry, wanted to know when supper would be ready, and then curtly withdrew.

Tom set to work quickly as he could at getting on with his cooking, and when the men and Woodhouse came in soon after everything was ready, and in fact the place looked brighter than usual,—all that better and nobler life in Tom was creeping to the surface.

In the evening began the first lesson in Catechism. Tom was fighting against that unwieldy ignorance around and within him; and as in polishing the rough diamond the rough exterior has to be worn away, and then the true brilliancy of the stone flashes through the dull outer case, so as the darkness of Tom's ignorance was lightened, the sweetness and truth of his natural disposition shone forth in deeds, not words. But Tom required, like everybody else in this work-a-day world, to be understood.

Tom bravely worked through the twelve articles of the Creed in his Catechism, and began studying the Sacraments, and then his wish grew to go to the Mission to receive the Sacrament of Penance, and having a great desire also to receive the Holy Sacrament, it was thought an Instruction from one of the Fathers would do him good. On one Sunday, ever memorable to Tom, he started (Woodhouse staying at home to do the Ranche work) on horseback for the Mission, with the one thought of carrying out this intention. Tom being brisk and getting his early work done, came in to dress and have the wants of his wardrobe supplied.

"I shall get through with my catechism if I remembers Sacraments and numbers of Persons in God."

"Ah, Tom, after all my trouble, don't split on that

11

rock," replied his friend, at the same time giving him a letter to Quinlin.

Towards evening Tom rode back crest-fallen. He could not go to the Sacraments, and quietly went about his work half broken-hearted.

A letter explained this. Let us look over the reader's shoulder to have the mystery explained. It had evidently been written hastily in pencil, and ran thus:

"DEAR YOUNG FRIEND,

Your protégé came to me this morning, and I examined him in his Catechism. To my astonishment, in asking him how many Persons are there in God? he replied, after careful consideration, 'seven.' How could I hear his confession under the circumstances? Will you instruct him anew, and send him to me again?

Yours very truly,

FATHER QUINLIN."

Nobody knows how much time had already been spent on Tom; only those about him saw with sorrow that he was too disheartened to attempt that journey to the Mission in a hurry again.

That evening the talk at the Ranche fell on the subject of Osages and Indian customs; about the Indians kindling a fire on every new tomb during four consecutive nights after a person's decease.

"That lights 'em up to the country of souls," said Hecker.

"I don't believe it," replies Tom.

"All I know is as how the Indians believes it," re-iterated Hecker. And as for you, why you ask one of the Fathers, they'll explain all about the legend to you. It's a long and beautiful story, Sir; I heard it amongst the Chippeways; and as for that," observed the speaker, "Why, fire I've heard say was always sacred. Why, the Vestal Virgins kept perpetual fire alight. The Jews even burn a lamp in the room in which a person dies, and place a little basin and a cloth by the body, for the soul to purify herself; and I've heard tell that in some countries in Europe on All Souls' day, the Cemeteries are covered with lamps, burning on the graves. It's true, ain't it, Sir?"

"Yes, a good deal of what you say is true, Hecker," replied Woodhouse, who was thinking deeply.

CHAPTER XX.

"Yet strange sights in truth I witness,
And I gaze until I tire;
Wondrous pictures, changing ever,
As I look into the fire."

Proctor.

FIRE WORSHIP—THE IGNICOLISTS.

IT was recreation hour at the Mission, and the Fathers were sitting in the room of the old Superior. Woodhouse, who had gone down to the Mission for letters, was with them.

"Will any of you," he asked, "tell me about Fire Worship amongst the Indians?"

They all had something to say on the subject, and on returning to the Ranche he made the following notes from the Fathers' conversation, which I insert here.

The worship of fire was very ancient in all their Indian tribes. In all their traditions it was found; and scarcely to be wondered at, considering the Greeks adored fire under the name of *Haitos*, and the Latins under the name of *Vesta*.

The ancient tribes of Natchez kept up continual fire in all their medicine lodges and temples. In New Mexico, old men of the Moquis tribe constantly keep up the sacred fire; should they sleep or allow the fire to be extinguished they believe unheard-of sufferings will come upon the whole Tribe. The Mexicans consecrated each one of the eighteen months in their year to a particular God, whom they honored with solemn festas and human sacrifices. Their tenth month (Xocolh huetzi) began about the fourth of August, and was consecrated to the God of Fire (Xuchten-hetli) with great feasting and human sacrifices. Living men were placed in the flames; half burnt, and still breathing, their hearts were torn out in presence of the Image of the God. In the centre of the court a lofty tree was planted, and round this tree they performed a thousand ceremonies and sacrifices worthy of their God.

The 18th month (Itzcali), near January the 12th, was dedicated to another Feast of Fire. About the 10th, in the middle of the night, they kindled *a new fire* before the Idol of the God, which was gorgeously apparelled. From this fire they lighted a grand pile. Hunters brought all they had killed or fished from the waters, and the priest cast it into the furnace. All the assistants were obliged to eat scalding-hot, tiny loaves of corn-meal, containing a portion of roast meat called Tamalillos. On this festival, for three years in succession no *human sacrifices* were offered, but on the fourth year the number of victims surpassed that of all other festivals. The king and his lords presented themselves in the midst of this heap of corpses to dance; and ludicrously grouped they all sang the *Neteuhicuicaliztli, or reserved chant.*

In a "Treatise on the Idolatry and Superstitions of the Mexicans," a manuscript, of 1629, we find what particularly attracted the veneration of the Mexicans was fire. For this reason that element presided at the birth, and almost all the actions of life. At the time of a child's birth, fire was kindled in the room of the mother, and kept up four consecutive days without removing any of it. They believed if the living coals were drawn out, a film would appear over the eyes of the new-born child. On the fourth day the child and the fire were taken out of the chamber; the fire was carried four times round the child's head, twice in one direction and twice in the opposite direction. At this time the child received its name, which was generally that of the element or animal to which the day was consecrated—as the alligator, serpent, eagle, tiger, or the fire, water, &c. In most of their sacrifices, tapers and incense had a place.

Chipiapoos* or *the Dead-man* is the great Manitou

---

* Longfellow has embodied this legend of Chipiapoos in his poem "Hiawatha," ascribing it to a Plagiarist, who copied it from the "Oregon Missions," p. 285, "by De Smet." At least, so says the Editor of one of De Smet's works. In the Tauchnitz edition of Longfellow (1856), Longfellow refers to a Mr. Schoolcraft for an account of Chiabo, (*Algic Researches*, Vol. 1, p. 134), and in his *History, Condition, and Prospects of the Indian Tribes of the United States*, part iii., p. 314, is the Iroquois form of the Tradition, derived verbally from an Onondaga chief.

according to the Potawatomies who presides in the country of souls, and maintains a sacred fire for all of his race who arrive there. Fire is in all the Indian Tribes an emblem of happiness and good fortune. Fire is lighted before all their deliberations. To *extinguish an enemy's fire* signifies to have gained a victory. They attribute to fire a sacred character, which is remarkable everywhere in their usages and customs, especially in religious ceremonies. Mysterious ideas are maintained concerning the nature and phenomena of fire, which is considered supernatural.

Before consulting a manitou or tutelary spirit, or before addressing the dead, fire is kindled. This fire is struck from flint ; it would be a grievous sin to light the sacred fire with common fire.

The Chippeways burn a fire on every new grave for four nights. By the light of this sacred fire the spirit journeys on its solitary and silent passage to the country of souls. The legend concerning this fire will be found elsewhere. One of the Fathers, in a visit to the Crows, then camped at the base of the Rocky Mountains, was an object of extreme veneration amongst the savages. He carried a box of phosphoric matches in the pocket of his cassock ; with these he used to light his pipe and their calumet. Fire, in a sensible or collective state, is well known to be one of the grandest agents of nature ; and for this very reason, perhaps, was regarded amongst most nations, in an early period of the world, either as the Creator and productive cause of all things, or, at least, as the substance from which the Creator produced all things. Hence, the Persians, Ethiopians, Scythians, and Carthagenians in the old world, and the Mexicans, Peruvians, and Indians in the new world, paid divine honors to the fire itself. Zoroaster ordained the erection of pyrea or temples dedicated to fire throughout all Persia. Even the Hebrews imagined fire to be the grandest proof of the presence of the Deity. Under this symbol God appeared to Moses on Mount Horeb, and to the Hebrews at large on Mount Sinai, on the promulgation of the Sacred Law; and under this symbol he evinced His protective presence every night, by assuming the form of a fiery pillar. Impressed with this idea, the Jews were ever anxious to preserve it in a pure and active flame upon the national altar; when, therefore, the Jews were borne away in captivity to Persia, the priests took the sacred fire of the altar and concealed it in a dry cave, with which none but themselves were acquainted, and where on their restoration to liberty, the posterity of those priests found it on their return to Judea (Maccab. ii. 1, 18). Fire was regarded with an equal degree of veneration throughout Greece and Rome. Temples in every city were erected to Vesta,* a name importing fire, whether

---

* Vesta, a goddess daughter of Rhea and Saturn. When considered as the Mother of the Gods, she is the mother of Rhea and Saturn; when considered as the Patroness of Vestal Virgins and the Goddess of Fire, she is called the daughter of Saturn and Rhea. Æneas first introduced her mysteries into Italy, and Numa built her a temple, in which no males were permitted to enter. A fire was kept continually

derived from the Greek or the Hebrew, and in every temple a lambent flame was perpetually burning over the altar.

As late even as the third century of the Christian era, when Heliogabalus anticipated his own apotheosis, and instituted the worship of himself all over the Roman Empire, having erected a magnificent Temple to his own divinity, he supplied its altar with sacred fire from the Temple of Vesta, which he stole for this purpose.

One cannot therefore be surprised to find this fire worship so prevalent amongst the Indian tribes. The grandeur of Catholic Ceremonial, drawing as it does to the worship of God, all that external of worship which was harmless in itself, yet symbolical and beautiful in Pagan Rites, has kept up that lambent flame before the Altar,† in the Sanctuary lamp, burning before the Holy

---

lighted in her sanctuary by a certain number of Virgins who were dedicated to the service of the goddess. As the Greeks and Romans were not so much given to worshipping stars as the Eastern nations, they adored Vesta and Vulcan, as the terrestrial and elementary fire, distinguishing the fire of the earth from that of heaven; taking Vesta for the earth, in the centre of which (according to their opinion) an eternal fire was burning. This is reported by Ovid in his Fasti, and this poet tells us afterwards that the perpetual fire they had was the only image of Vesta, it being impossible to have a true image of fire. It was customary formerly to keep a fire at the entry of houses, which therefore has ever since kept the name of Vestibule (Vestibulum). Formerly in this entry those who lived in the house sat at long tables to take their meals, where fire represented the gods.

† Blessing in the porch of her churches on Holy Saturday new fire, struck from the flint, and from this fire all lamps and candles are lit in the Church, and this fire is not supposed to die out throughout the year.

Sacrament. Also, she has upon her Altars those six large candlesticks round the Tabernacle that the people may follow the vision of the eagle-eyed Evangelist and see as it were six candlesticks, and one in between them like unto the Son of Man.

And of those tongues of flame that lit on Apostolic brows ?

The use of lights in the service of the Jewish Temple is a fact too well authenticated to require proof, such is the historical celebrity, both religious and profane, belonging to the seven-branched candlestick which the Almighty God Himself commanded to be made according to the pattern shown to Moses in the Mount. (Exod. c. xxv., v. 31.)

But these notes are growing too long. They are but thoughts thrown together to make others search out the strange sights and changing pictures that group round every fire-side. The further study of this subject will, I hope, while away some few hours of my readers in the coming winter evenings.

CHAPTER XXI.

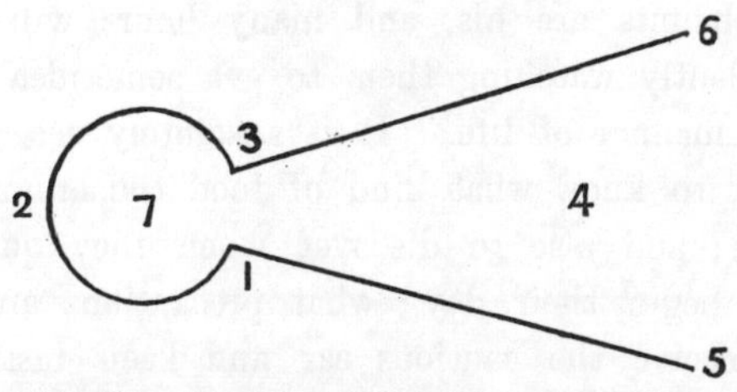

Plan of Indian Buffalo Pen.—1, 2, 3, Pen ; 1, 3, Opening ; 4, Slope ;
1, 5 and 3, 6, Hills and Fences ; 7, Medicine Post.

BUFFALO HUNT.

ON the broad Prairie hunting is the one thought
of all tribes of the Indians. Their *summum
bonum* in life is to be a good hunter and
a good warrior. These are the credentials to savage
nobility, these qualities constitute a man being called
a great man amongst the wandering tribes of North
America.

Directly the babe leaves his mother's arms his first
toy is a little bow, and his play consists in hunting
small birds and animals. The knowledge the Indians
obtain of the nature and instinct of animals is truly

marvellous. The young Indians are initiated in all their
stratagems, they are taught *with more care* how to
approach and kill animals than English children are
taught reading, writing, languages and dancing.   An
expert Indian hunter is acquainted minutely with the
habits and instincts of all animals usually hunted. Their
favourite haunts are his, and many hours will he lay
hidden, silently watching them to get some idea of their
ways and manner of life.   It is absolutely necessary for
the hunter to know what kind of food the animals seek,
and when; and also to discover when they quit their
lairs, and begin their day ; what precautions are necessary to deceive the cautious ear and keen instincts of
the victim he intends hunting down. He has to study
the foot-fall in the long grass, or in the woodlands,
calculate the length of time since it passed, think out
what direction it could go in. And all this the Indian
does with a sagacity that surprises Europeans.

In the great book of Nature he is perpetually studying
whilst in pursuit of his game.   The atmosphere, the
wind, rain, snow, ice, the forests, the creeks and lakes
are the books the Indian consults.

The buffalo, or bison, supplies almost all the necessaries of life to the Indian. Out of buffalo skins they
make lodges, or Indian houses. The skins also furnish
clothing, litters, bridles and saddle cloths, vessels to hold
water, boats to cross lakes and rivers ; whilst from the
hair they make their cordage; from the sinews, bow-
strings, thread for their clothes and glue. The bones

serve for implements—the shoulder-blade is both spade and pick-axe. The bison is the daily bread of the Indian, in fact his only chief food.

The dung of the buffalo (bois-de-vache) supplies abundant fuel. Before the whites encroached on the Prairies, the method of killing the different animals consisted chiefly in *stratagems* and *snares*. Even now the Indians resort to that primitive method whilst hunting large animals, when their horses are weak and incapable of pursuing them, or when their powder and shot fall short. The trap prepared for the bison is an enclosure or carel, and is one of the primitive ways and perhaps the most remarkable in its execution. It has existed from time immemorial; forsooth it requires skill, and when once seen a high idea is formed of Indian sagacity, activity and hardiesse. As on all the grand occasions of life the jugglers or medicine men are consulted, they are not wanting to the hunt, for it is preceded by a great variety of superstitious practices.

We are going to assist at a hunt at the base of the Rocky Mountains. Bisons roam the broad Prairies of the West in herds of several hundreds, and often of several thousands. Travelling through these great plains one sees thousands of these noble animals moving quietly, browsing in seemingly interminable troops. They look very fearful; their great hairy heads would strike terror into any one ignorant of the pacific habits of the poor beast. So great is their timidity that a single man can put to fright the most numerous herd; when frightened, their prolonged bellowings, the tramp of their feet and the dust they raise resemble some grand tempest, with its deep murmurings, its pealings of thunder, and strong gusts of wind carrying with it clouds of dust.

Bison flesh is much esteemed on account of its nourishing qualities. But to our Assiniboin Buffalo Hunt. The Indians encamped on a suitable spot for the construction of an enclosure ; their camp contained between two or three thousand souls, and some three hundred lodges. With great forethought they had selected the base of a chain of hills, which gently sloping formed a narrow, almost hidden valley, and a small Prairie in which all the lodges were ranged. Opposite the hills, in all its grandeur, stretched far away the broad Prairie. The construction of the lodges was speedily got over ; then was held a solemn Council, at which all the Chiefs and the Hunters assisted. They chose a band of warriors to hinder the hunters from leaving the camp, either by themselves or in detached companies, for fear they should disturb the bison, and drive them away from the environs of the encampment. All the Indians of the camp are obliged to conform to this law. In case any one belonging to the camp should transgress this law, their guns are confiscate, their bows and arrows broken, their lodges cut in pieces, their dogs killed, and all provisions and hides are taken from them ; should they resist, they are beaten with sticks, bows, and clubs, and this torment frequently ends in death. Any one setting fire to the Prairie by accident or imprudence, or who should in any way frighten the herd, would be sure to be well beaten.

'Directly this law is circulated in the camp, the building of the pen commences. It is a pleasure to see with what cheerful ardour they labour; it is an affair of no common interest; their meals for many a day depend upon the success they now have, for the food they now seek must last the tribe for several months.

The enclosure shuts in about an acre. To make it circular they fix stakes in the ground firmly, between the stakes they weave dry boughs, make barricades with logs, bring together masses of stone; in fine, anything that will prevent a buffalo escaping answers their purpose. This round enclosure has but one opening; before this opening is a slope embracing fifteen or twenty feet between the hills; this inclined plane grows wider as it diverges from the circle; at its two sides the fence is built up a long way into the plain.

As quickly as they can get everything ready, the Indians elect a grand-master of ceremonies and of the enclosure. Generally he is an old man, distinguished for some feats of bravery, belonging to a *Wah-Kon*, or medicine band, famous in arts of jugglery, which the Indians deem a supernatural science. Ex-officio, he is to decide the moment of driving the buffaloes into the enclosure, and give the signal for the beginning of the hunt. It is this M. C. who plants the medicine mast in the centre of the park, and attaches to it the mystic charms which are to draw to this centre that hairy band, roaming in freedom not far off.   Let us look at his charms.

A streamer of crimson cloth, two or three yards long, a piece of tobacco, and a bison's horn, and the Manitous, or guiding spirits of the buffaloes, in order to discover the propitious moment for the chase signal to be given.

This royal master of ceremonies has four runners at his sole disposal; these he sends out daily, and they report to him each evening the observations they have made: they let him know at what distance from the camp the animals are feeding, their probable number, and the direction they are marching in. These runners often go forty to forty-five miles in different directions.   In all their journeys they take with them the wah-kon ball, which is entrusted to them by this worthy Master of Ceremonies. This ball is made of hair and covered with skin; when the runners think the suitable moment has come, they immediately send a man of their number to the M. C. with the ball and the good news. As long as that mysterious ball is absent, the Master of the Ceremonies can take no food; the only break to this rigorous fast is when some game or animal is killed on the enclosure, and this belongs to the M. C. As they have been known to remain a month awaiting the favourable moment, the grand-master must find himself reduced to small rations. He has, however, no more appearance of fasting than his brethren have in the camp, notwithstanding his meagre rations; therefore I incline to think, with others, he makes some arrangement with his conscience—stealthily, and in the darkness of night. But the longest day has an evening, the longest lane a turning, and an end comes to the rigorous faster's fast.

The rolling of a drum breaks the deep stillness of the camp. What anxiety on the part of the Indian population! Ah! Yes, it is he! It is the grandmaster of the enclosure. He announces in sonorous tones that the bison are from fifteen to twenty miles distant from the camp; the wind is favourable, it blows directly from the buffaloes' feeding ground. In how short a time does the stagnant waiting of the camp change to that deep joyousness evinced in the Indian chase. Immediately the horsemen mount their coursers; the foot soldiers arm themselves with bows, guns, and lances, and speedily take up their position —forming two long, oblique, diverging rows from the extremity of the two barriers which spring from the the entrance of the pen, and extend far out into the plain, and thus they prolong indefinitely the diverging lines of the enclosure. The foot-men are placed at distances of from ten to fifteen feet, the horsemen continue the same lines, which separate in proportion as they extend, so that the last hunter on horseback is found at about two or three miles distance from the

pen, and at very nearly the same distance from the
last hunter of the other line in an opposite direction.
Should men be wanting, even women and children
occupy stations.   After the formation of these immense, far-extending lines, one Indian only, alone,
unarmed, is sent upon the best courser in the camp
in the direction of the buffaloes, to meet them. Watch
him. How swiftly he proceeds, how he draws near to
them against the wind ; what a study that precaution !
Ah, he knows upon his shoulders rests a heavy burden,
upon his action depends a nation's food for many
months to come.   Will he be successful ?   Ah, well,
in watching him one feels the crimson dust within
one's frame pulsate more quickly ; in that intense
straining silence one almost imagines the loud throb
of one's own heart will chase the herd away, and one
presses one's hand over the heart to still its beating.
See how quickly, at the distance of about one hundred
paces from them, he envelopes himself in a buffalo
hide, the fur turned outwards, and at the same time
horse and rider appear clothed in the same manner. O,
quick beating heart, what is that plaintive cry breathing out upon the air ? The imitation of the cry of
a lost bison calf. Surely, oh, surely, that cry is too
natural to be human. Look closer. As if by enchant-
ment that cry attracts the attention of the whole herd ;
yet only a few seconds, and several hundreds of these
quadrupeds—hearing that low pitiful wail, something
so lost, so broken-hearted, stealing on the air—turn

towards the pretended calf. Oh, herd, beware. At first they move slowly, then advance into a trot, and at last break into full unwieldly gallop. The horseman without ceasing repeats the cry of the calf, and takes his course towards the pen, ever watching to keep that equal distance from the animals that press hard upon him. Strange stratagem thus to lead so many from that vast herd of buffaloes through the whole distance separating him from his companions, who, watching with pale faces and beating hearts, impatiently long to join in the sport.

When the buffaloes gallop into the space between the extremities of the two lines the scene changes. All assumes an appearance of eagerness; hunters on horseback, giving rein to their steeds, rejoin each other, thus re-uniting those vastly converging lines; thus meeting behind the animals.

Then commences the panic in the great herd. The wind blowing from the rear, the scent of the hunters is communicated amongst the frightened and routed animals, who in every way attempt to regain their freedom—useless indeed now those on foot appear. The buffaloes finding themselves surrounded on all sides, excepting the single opening into the circular pen before them, low and bellow, and shriek out the maddening fear that has come upon them, and plunge into the open space of the pen with the untired speed of fear and desperation. Gradually the line of hunters close in behind them, and space becomes less necessary as the mass of buffaloes and the hunters become more and more compact. What deafening firing of guns! what twanging of bows! what swift drawing forth of arrows! what flinging of lances! Many animals fall under the shot, the blows, and the arrows, before reaching the pen; the greater number enter. Poor brute beasts, you discover, too late, the snare laid so skilfully for you. Those in front try to return, but the terrified crowd following, forces them forward, and in inextricable confusion do they find themselves in the enclosure, amidst wild, prolonged hurrahs, and fierce, uncontrolled shouting of the whole waiting tribe, intermingled with the continuous firing of guns.

Penned now, poor innocents, the carnage is swift and steady, as they fall beneath arrows, lances, and knives. What wild excitement of joy in savage natures! What general butchery! What flaying and cutting up of animals! Can any one look on without disgust?

Yes! those habituated to their customs and manners. Men of those western plains cut and slash into that mass of flesh. Ah, horror!—women, and innocent pretty Indian children in particular, devour meat warm with life! Livers, kidneys, brains, seem attractions impossible to resist.

'Tis a feast — a wild carnage of blood. For, see! they smear their faces, their hair, their arms and legs with this warm sweet buffalo blood!

What confusion of cries, as of Babel! what clamourous shouts! whilst here and there do quarrels fill up the scene.

It is picturesque if you will. It is savage. It is a very pandemonium. Words fail to depict such a sight. What pen and ink painting can give warm life to such disgusting details, this carnage of six hundred odd bison ?

Now it is evening. The butchery is finished, the skins lay in their heaps, the flesh lies in its piles ; and now comes the division of the chase amongst the families, in proportion to the numbers composing them. The meat then is cut into slices and dried ; the bones are bruised, and the grease extracted.

The dogs of the wigwams receive their share of the feast, and their festival hall is the arena of the pen where so much noise and slaughter has reigned.

But forty-eight hours, and no vestige of that carnage remains.

On this site several days are passed in dancing and mirth, and then comes the separation of the Indian families.

If one of the great masters of the olden world could but assist at such a scene in the great Western Desert, what a painting would come into life !

Such scenes as these will vanish into the dead-gone years, as the swift foot of European civilization crushes out Indian life. In the quick future it will be but as a dream that is told.

CHAPTER XXII.

"Lo, how all things fade and perish ;
From the memory of the old men,
Fade away the great traditions."—*Longfellow.*

GRASSHOPPER HUNT AMONGST THE SOSHOCOS.

ON'T look surprised ; it is at a grasshopper hunt I invite you to assist with us to-day, a grasshopper hunt amongst the Soshocos."

Imagine finding a note like that lying on your breakfast table, or the place where your breakfast table should be on the Prairie trail. Forgetting self, let us go.

Who are these Soshocos ? A tribe of Indians, the most degraded of all the races of the vast western world. They roam over the desert, and barren districts of Utah and California, and all about that part of the Rocky Mountains branching into Oregon.

The Indians of the plains living on nourishing flesh of buffaloes are generally pretty tall, active, robust, and clad in skins. These Soshocos, who subsist chiefly on grasshoppers and ants, are miserable, lean, weak, and as a rule badly clothed ; they inspire sentiments of compassion in all those who travel through the unproductive region they occupy.

Nearly all the Soshoco territory is covered with Wormwood, and species of Artemesia, in which the grasshoppers swarm in myriad numbers; these parts are consequently most frequented by this tribe. When they are sufficiently numerous they hunt together. They begin by digging a hole ten or twelve feet long, by four or five feet deep; then, armed with long branches of artemesia, they surround a field of four or five acres, more or less. The distances they stand apart vary, according to the number of people engaged in the hunt.

They are generally about twenty feet apart, and their whole work is to beat the ground, so as to frighten up the grasshoppers and make them jump forwards. They chase them towards the centre by degrees, that is, into the hole prepared for their reception. Grasshoppers abound so in this district that three or four acres furnish grasshoppers sufficient to fill the reservoir or hole.

There the Soshocos will stay as long as the provision lasts. What a queer taste they have! Bah, grasshopper soup! grasshoppers boiled! grasshoppers roasted! Yet here the poor Soshoco sits watching a grasshopper roast. He takes a pointed stick and threads the larger grasshoppers on it, then fixes the rod in the ground before the fire; as they become roasted they are broken off, until the whole are devoured. But there is another sort of grasshopper cookery. A group yonder are crushing grasshoppers between large stones, and making a kind of paste with them; this they flavour with herbs and dry in the sun, or before the fire. That will serve for winter provision.

As the buffalo is the daily bread of most tribes, so

is the grasshopper the daily bread of this tribe, for they scarcely ever trouble themselves to kill deer, or large animals, although at rare intervals they meet with rabbits, or kill a few grouse.

Grasshoppers and locusts do a great deal of mischief in some of the States. In great flocks they seem to devour all things green before them, and should they pass over a railroad when a train is coming, the train inevitably comes to a standstill. This is attributed to their containing in their bodies a kind of oil; they form so thickly on the rails, that the engine-wheels passing over their bodies, after a while get so saturated with oil that they are powerless to lay hold of the line, and so rotate without advancing.

Note. Travelling from Maisons-sur-Seine up to Paris with an English Roman Catholic Bishop, well known for his enjoyment of a hearty joke, in the midst of a conversation upon travelling in general, accidents, and stoppages, &c., one of the two Ecclesiastics with him said he had been in a train stopped by grasshoppers. The Bishop stoutly denied the possibility of such an occurrence, when fortunately for the Ecclesiastic's veracity, some Americans in the same compartment assured his Lordship that this occurred often in some States subject to grasshopper ravages. That they themselves had several times been in trains thus temporarily arrested on their course. Europeans often accuse Americans of "drawing a strong bow" on these questions, but like many things else in life, a little sifting of the subject-matter shows how much truth lies at the bottom of the remark. "A train stopped by grasshoppers" sounds oddly enough, and yet knowing Caseline oil poured on the iron-way will stop a train, and also by analysis knowing that a fatty oil-like substance, with somewhat of the Caseline property about it, exists in the body of the grasshopper, the difficulty immediately ceases as to the possibility of such a thing happening—given a sufficient quantity of grasshoppers to produce the required amount of oil. Europeans once seeing grasshoppers in shoals, would find the laugh on the Americans' side against their incredulity.

CHAPTER XXIII.

"Then the black robe chief, the prophet,
  Told his message to the people,
  Told the purport of his mission,
  Told them of the Virgin Mary,
  And her blessed Son, the Saviour,
  How in distant lands and ages
  He had lived on earth as we do;
  How he fasted, prayed, and laboured;
  How the Jews, the tribe accursed,
  Mocked him, scourged him, crucified him;
  How he rose from where they laid him,
  Walked again with his disciples,
  And ascended into Heaven."—*Longfellow.*

MASS ON THE PRAIRIES.

THERE is a sound of strange melody disturbing the perpetual stillness of the prairies; broken seldom but by the soft susurra of the breeze sweeping gently over the prairie grass and spring flowers. There is a little tent upon the prairie, and underneath it an Altar, and at its Altar a Priest; and kneeling out into the sweet sunshine are swarthy forms—Indians—who themselves have decked that Table of the Lord, with the richest and brightest prairie flowers they can find, and who now await His coming in the Sacramental Feast, whose blessed feet so many years ago walked upon the waves of this troublesome world. Rejoice, O Prairie, thy King cometh!

The lights flicker solemnly within the tent, the words of the Creed are monotonéd by the Indians; then the Lord's prayer, and the Ave. How strangely those words break the stillness of the Prairie!

Hawai Marie Wagkonda odikupi odishailow
Hail, Mary, of the Great Spirit of gifts thou art

wagkonda shodigue acchow. Wakoki odisanha
the great spirit with thee is. The women among whom

odichoupegtsiow. Jusus tsaitse ouglagran ingshe
thou art blessed. Jesus of the womb the fruit thy

ougoupegtsiow. Wâlâgui Marie Wagkonda ehonh
is blessed. Holy Mary of the Great Spirit the mother

wawatapiow, dekousi antzapi aitchanski.
pray for us, now and at the moment of our death.

Aikougtsiou.
Amen.

And now upon the hearts of some rests that same Holy Food once distributed to a few beloved ones in an upper room by the Holiest of all Holy Hands. Methinks that susurra causes the prairie grass to bow itself in honour of Him. O, simple service, with faithful believing hearts around. Grander art thou than the most gorgeous ceremonial under the dome of S. Peter's, or under the roof of the Lateran Basilica. Nobler is that officiating Priest, bowed down by self-denial, by the self-sacrifice of a whole life, than many a courtly Ecclesiastic with flowing robes and worldly mien, such as one sees listlessly performing duties in many a stately Church in the old world. Before the vision then there arises that simple old man on his far Prairie Mission.

Surely such an one as this Prairie Priest teaches all of us by his life *that religion* pure and undefiled before God the Father,—that safer keeping of ourselves un-spotted from the world. Dearer to that good old man are those guttural Indian sounds than the weeping tones of the *Miserere* creeping through the Sistina those mourning days of Holy Week; dearer than the jubilant Credo or Gloria echoing up into and dying away in the broad roof of S. Peter's on Easter-Day.

It is no fancy; he himself has confessed it.

CHAPTER XXIV.

> " God's world has one great echo ;
>   Whether calm blue mists are curled,
>   Or lingering dew-drops quiver,
>   Or red storms are unfurled ;
>   The same deep love is throbbing
>   Through the great heart of God's world."
>
> *Proctor.*

WASHING DAY—RANCHE LIFE AGAIN.

RANCHE life had resumed the old swing at Kirwan's. Charley was back from his wearisome journey, and his father and mother were coming on this day to visit the Ranche—a sacred place to them, hallowed by Brown's death. The Ranche boys were up earlier that day, off at their work ; Tom and Woodhouse were getting the Ranche in order ; and Charley Kirwan himself was putting up a new bedstead in the one living-room.

" I think you'll like them, old fellow ; they know all about you, and how Brown liked you, and they come out West prepared to like you, so it will be easy cantering over the ground of introduction."

" I only hope one thing, that they will enjoy your

quiet, primitive life as well as I did before the epidemic came."

"I hope so too," replied Charley, with one of his sunny smiles. "I told them if they would stay on out here for some months, for a change, I would build another room off the Ranche on purpose for their accommodation."

"Rather rough lines for a lady, is it not, coming out as it is?"

"My mother is a woman who always grasps the position of life, wherever it may be. Why, bless you, man, she'll be teaching us how to cook and wash, and enjoy doing it. But good-bye, I'm off to fetch them here. According to my arrangements they slept at the Mission Hotel last night."

Towards sunset Charley came back to the Ranche, bringing his father and mother and his brother-in-law to supper. It was only the ordinary supper, but the table looked brighter than usual, as Woodhouse had gathered bunches of large crimson gladioli-like flowers from the Creek, and other gorgeous prairie blooms, to give somewhat of an air of civilization to the homeliness of the place.

As Charley's mother came in she gave a start, perceptible only to those quick eyes watching her. She grasped the hand of Woodhouse, whilst only three words escaped her lips: "My son's friend." The quick nervous fingers lingered in his, and a friendship seemed to grow out of the clasp. She had a kind word for all the

Ranche boys, seeming innately to know the words best suited to each.

And Charley's father showed age well preserved. He was quiet, gentlemanly, kind ; a man whom one would imagine only spoke after thought, and thought well thought out.

The brother-in-law was a jolly American, who loved shooting, and who was eager for news about prairie chickens, ducks, quails, and so forth.

As usual with Americans, they soon grew into the Prairie life, and a pleasant evening was spent, chatting round the fire ; late as they sat up, the evening did not seem to grow old, nor the time hang wearily.

The following day was given up entirely to a visit to the Upper Ranche, travelling in an ox waggon over the Prairie, with chairs to sit upon, and a well-filled lunch basket in their midst, whilst every now and again Charley and his brother-in-law left the waggon to have a shot at some quail or prairie chicken near the track. It was an early spring day, but the golden sunshine was not too hot—just such a day as would make any one love the great expanse of Prairie, and joy in it ; and delighted with these Western Plains, they drove right up to the great herd of cattle that Charley owned. A look of surprise seemed to creep over the faces of the new-comers to see Charley's great wealth. They had heard before of his being a man who owned a vast herd, yet evidently Charley was not a prophet in his own country, or amongst his own people.

The lunch basket was opened now, and, watching the herd grazing, they took their luncheon. More enjoyable the contents of that lunch basket seemed than any lunch basket on an English course. The Ranche boys of the Upper Ranche, riding close up to the waggon sides, had their share of the feast too.

A dinner was speedily got ready at the Upper Ranche, and some wild duck shot on the Upper Creek, a basket of wild grapes picked in the wood bordering the Creek, and then came an enjoyable drive home, which was reached in the gloaming.

* * * *

It was washing-day. at the Ranche. Mrs. Kirwan had suggested it, and volunteered a lesson; and so on the great fire in the Ranche was a large collection of saucepans, and on the stove kettles boiling, so that they should have hot water sufficient for such a festival. Meanwhile, two wash-tubs were in full swing, with two helpers at each; and merry peals of laughter rang through the small house; clouds of steam filled the room, and the nostrils were assailed by that sweet, healthy scent of soap-suds. Out in the sunshine, on lines, the clean white linen was drying and flying in the Prairie breeze; and to the amusement of all, who should ride up on horseback but the old Superior of the Mission; so dinner had to be got ready, and it was high festival indeed. Mrs. Kirwan looked none the less a lady with her hands in the wash-tub, and Charley and Woodhouse scrubbed with a will. It was such a living, animated picture, that no one with heart in them could shrink from participating in it. The laughter rippling away from the wash-tubs out into the clear sunshine, and the "Now am I right, Mrs. Kirwan?" and the "Will you tell me this, Mrs. Kirwan?" and the "Bravo! Bravo!" of the old Superior, filling up the crevices of the running conversation, was something too enjoyable of Ranche life to be passed over without a word.

And then the starching and ironing, the perpetual failure, the little success in that department, and also the final consignment of all of that department to Mrs. Kirwan. And the guests thought the dinner twice as good as usual, because Mrs. Kirwan suggested this or that—"Shouldn't the ducks be stuffed with onions?" or "Wouldn't this be nice?" It seemed one long-continued picnic, in the warmth of which the dear, staid old man from the Mission grew young again. Perchance his far Belgian home grew up before his memory, and the happy days of childhood, when in the farm-yard kitchen he had seen like ways.

The Kirwans were leaving in a few weeks, and Woodhouse was also going North; sorry, all of them, that the curtain was about to fall over the Rancher's Home.

CHAPTER XXV.

"Ye who love a nation's legends,
Love the ballads of a people
That like voices from afar off
Call to us, to pause and listen,
Speak in tones so plain and child-like,
Scarcely can the ear distinguish,
Whether they are sung or spoken—
Listen to this Indian legend.
   *   *   *   *
Where he passed, the branches moved not;
Where he trod, the grasses bent not:
And the fallen leaves of last year
Made no sound beneath his footsteps."

Longfellow.

CHIPPEWAY FIRE LEGENDS.

THE origin of sacred and funereal fire amongst the Chippeways engrossed the attention of all at the Ranche. The following fire legend is the result of their researches.

A war party of Chippeways met some enemies in a large and beautiful plain. The war whoop rang out, and a fierce contest began. The Chippeway Chief was a very distinguished warrior; in this fight he surpassed himself in bravery, and a great number of enemies

13

fell beneath the redoubled blows of his tomahawk. He was giving the signal for shouting the cry of victory when he received an arrow in his breast, and fell lifeless amongst his braves. A warrior receiving his last blow in the act of combating is never buried. An ancient custom exists, and from this the tribe never depart—to seat a warrior thus falling on the battle field, his back resting against a tree, and his face turned in the direction which indicates the flight of his enemies. It was the case with this Chief. His grand crest of eagle's plumes was placed upon his head, for each feather denoted a trophy, or scalp won in combat. His face was carefully painted. He was clothed in his most costly habiliments, as though he were alive. All his equipments were picturesquely arranged by his side, his bow and his quiver of arrows resting against his shoulder. The *post of the brave* was planted in front of him with solemn ceremonies and with honours due only to illustrious warriors. The rites, the chants, the funereal speeches were celebrated according to the custom of his nation in similar circumstances. And then his companions offered him their farewells. No one had any doubt that he was dead—the sequel shows whether they were right.

Although deprived of speech and all other signs of life, the Chief heard distinctly the words of the songs, the discourses, the cries and the lamentations of his warriors. He witnessed their gestures, their dances, and all their ceremonies around the "post of honour."

His icy hand was sensible to their warm clasp of
farewell. His lips, pale and livid, felt the ardour and
heat of the farewell embrace and salute, and yet he
could not return it. Forsaken, knowing it, his anguish
was untold, and his desire grew strong to accompany
his braves back to their village. He saw them disappear in the dim distance, and then soul and body
fought for mastery. His agitated spirit made a violent
movement, and then he seemed to rise and follow them.
His spirit form was invisible — a new cause to him of
surprise and contradiction, and this swelled his grief
and untold despair. He followed them closely. Where
they went, he went also. When they marched, he marched.
Riding or on foot he was in their midst. He camped
with them. He slept by their side. He awoke with
them. All their fatigues, troubles, and labors he shared.
He enjoyed the pleasures of their conversation ; yet
whilst present at their meals, no drink was offered to
allay his thirst, no dishes to appease his hunger. Question and answer remained without response. "Warriors,
my braves," cried he in the bitterness of his anguish ;
"Do you not hear the voice of your chief? Look, do
you not see my form? You are motionless. You seem
not to see and hear me. Stanch the blood still flowing
from the deep wound I have received. Suffer me not
to die deprived of aid—to famish amidst abundance.
O, you braves, whom I often led in the thickest of
the fight, who have always been obedient to my voice,
already you seem to forget me ! Give me one drop

of water only to quench my feverish thirst, one mouthful of food to stay this gnawing hunger. In my distress how dare you refuse me ?"

At each halt he addressed them, alternately in reproach and pleading, but in vain. No one understood his words. If they heard his voice, it was only to them as the susurra of the wind sweeping over the great plains, or the murmurings of the summer breeze through the foliage and branches of the forests ; with them it remained unnoticed and unheeded.

After a long and painful journey, the war party arrived on the summit of a lofty eminence over-looking their villages. The warriors prepared to make their solemn entry. Decorated with their costliest ornaments, with faces carefully painted, and their victorious trophies attached to them, especially scalps fastened on to their bows, tomahawks, and lances, they burst forth into one unanimous cry of joy and victory, " Kumaudjeewug, Kumaudjeewug, Kumaudjeewug,"—*i. e.*, they have met, have fought, have conquered. The joyous shout resounded again and again throughout the whole camp. According to custom, the women and children came forth to meet the warriors in order to honor their return and sing their praises.

Those who had lost some member of their family approached with anxiety and eagerness to see if they were really dead, and to re-assure themselves that they died manfully, fighting against the enemy. Old men, bowed down with the weight of their years, consoled themselves for the loss of their sons if they sank like brave men, arms in hand ; the grief of the youthful widows loses its bitterness as they hear the praises bestowed on the names of their husbands. Thrilling recitals of combat awaken the martial fire in the bosoms of the youth; tiny children, incapable of understanding the joy of this grand festival, mingle their feeble shouts with the boisterous welcomes of the whole tribe.

Amidst all this clamour and rejoicing, no one knew of the presence of the great war-chief. He heard the information his own relations and friends received concerning his fortunes ; he heard the recital of his bravery ; he heard the singing of his lofty deeds ; he heard of his glorious death in the midst of vanquished enemies ; he heard of the *post of the brave* planted on the field of battle. " Here I am," cried he ; " I see, I walk,—look at me, touch me, I am not dead. Tomahawk in hand I shall renew my march against the enemy at the head of my braves, and soon in the banquet you will hear the beating of my drum."

No one heard him ; no one perceived him. The voice of the great Chief was no more to them than the perpetual din of the water falling from cascade to cascade at the foot of their village. Impatiently he took the direction of his lodge. There he found his wife in the greatest despair, cutting—in token of mourning — her long and floating locks ; lamenting bitterly her misfortune, the loss of a cherished husband,

and the desolate state of her orphan children. He strove to undeceive her. He breathed words of tenderness in her ear. He sought to clasp his children in his arms; but how vain, how futile his attempts. They were insensible to his voice and fatherly caresses. The mother, bathed in tears, sat inclining her head between her hands. The chief, suffering and dejected, besought her to dress his deep wound; to apply to it the herbs and roots contained in his medicine sack; but she moved not, she answered only with tears and groans. Then he placed his mouth close to the ear of his wife, and shouted aloud, "I am thirsty, I am hungry. Give me food and drink." The squaw thought she heard a rumbling in her ears, and spoke of it to her companions. The chief in his anger struck her a violent blow on her brow. She quietly pressed her hand to the stricken spot and said, "I feel a slight head-ache."

Frustrated at every step, and in all his efforts to make himself known, the great Chief began to reflect on what he had heard in his youth from the most distinguished jugglers he had met. They had told him that sometimes the spirit or soul quits the body, and wanders about according to its own pleasure and will. He then thought that possibly his body was lying on the field of battle, and that his spirit only had accompanied the warriors on their return to the village. In a moment he resolved to return by the same path he had come—a distance of four days' march. For the first three days he met no one. On the afternoon of the fourth, being close to the battle-field, he saw a fire near the path upon which he was walking. Wishing to avoid it, he quitted the track; but the fire at the same instant changed its position, and placed itself always in front of him. In vain he hurried from right to left. The same mysterious fire always preceded him, as if to bar his entrance to the field of battle. "I also," said he, "I am a spirit. I am seeking to return into my body. *I will* accomplish my design. Thou shalt purify me, but thou shalt not hinder me. I have always conquered my enemies, notwithstanding the greatest obstacles. This day *I will triumph over thee, spirit of fire.*" Having thus exclaimed, with an intense effort he darted towards the mysterious flame. He came forth from a long trance. He found himself seated on the battle ground, his back supported against a tree. His bow, his arrows, his clothes, his ornaments, his war accoutrements, the post of the brave; all were in the same position in which his braves had left them on the day of strife. He raised his eyes, and perceived a large eagle perched on the highest branch of a tree above his head. Immediately he recognised his manitou bird: the same that had appeared to him in his earlier life, when he came out of the days of childhood. It was the bird he had selected for his tutelary spirit, and of which he had always worn a talon suspended from his neck. His manitou had carefully guarded his body, and had prevented vultures and other birds of prey from devouring it. The Chief rose slowly, but found himself weak and reduced. The blood from his wound had ceased to flow, and he dressed it. He was well acquainted with the known healing power of certain leaves and roots. He sought them, gathering them with care in the forest, and, crushing some between two stones, applied them; others he chewed and swallowed.

After the lapse of a few weary days, he felt sufficient strength to attempt the return to his village; but hunger consumed him. In the absence of larger animals he lived on the little birds which his arrows brought down, and he varied his diet by eating insects and reptiles, also roots and berries. After many hardships he arrived on the banks of a river that separated him from wife, children and friends. The Chief uttered the shout agreed upon in such circumstances: the shout of the happy return of some absent friend. The signal was heard. A canoe was immediately sent for him. During the absence of the canoe conjectures were numerous concerning the absent person, whose friendly shout of approach had just been heard. All those who had been present in his warlike band were now in camp—the dead alone remained on the field of battle. "Might not the unknown on the other shore be an absent hunter, or might not this shout be the bold ruse of an enemy to take the scalps of the rowers?" Whilst all these conjectures are going on, the warlike chief embarks. He soon presents himself before them, amid the acclamations and joyful shouts of his relatives and friends.

The Indians eagerly pour forth from every lodge to shake hands with, and to celebrate the happy return of their chief and faithful conductor. That day was for them ever memorable and solemn. They returned thanks to the Great *Master of Life*, and to many Manitous of the Indian calendar. The whole day was consumed in dances, songs, and banquets.

When the first wave of astonishment and universal joy had died away, and somewhat of usual quiet was restored to the village, the Chief beat his drum in order to gather together his people. He told them the story of his strange adventure, and terminated his recital by making known to them and imposing upon them " the worship of the sacred and funereal fire," that is to say, the ceremony of maintaining for four consecutive nights a fire on every newly-closed sepulchre. He told them that this devotion is advantageous, and agreeable to the soul of the deceased ; that the journey to the country of souls is four long days ; that in this journey the soul needs a fire every night in its encampment ; that this funereal fire, kindled on the tomb by the near relatives of the deceased, serves to enlighten and warm the soul during its wanderings. The Chippeways believe that when this rite is neglected, the soul or spirit is forced to maintain a fire itself, and that with the greatest inconvenience.

CHAPTER XXVI.

"Ye who love the haunts of nature,
Love the sunshine of the meadow,
Love the shadow of the forest,
Love the wind amongst the branches,
And the rain-shower and the snow-storm,
And the rushing of great rivers
Through their palisades of pine trees,
And the thunder in the mountains,
Whose innumerable echoes
Flap like eagles in their eyries;
Listen to these wild traditions."—*Longfellow.*

THE LENNI-LENAPI, WAKA-TANKA, WAKA-CHEEKA.

THE Lenni-Lenapi have a peculiar idea of their first descendant, and the Missionary De Smet, in his studies of the Indian tribes, inserted this legend in his notes, having heard it from the mouth of Watomika the swift footed, or *celeripes.* They believe that a Great Spirit first created land and water, trees and plants, birds and fishes, animals and insects, and in the last place he created the first Lenap thuswise: He placed a snail on the shore of a large and beautiful river, which had its source in a far distant mountain, near to the rising sun. After twelve moons had rolled away the snail brought forth a red-skinned man. The Red-skin, discontented with his lonely lot, made a canoe of bark, and descended the river in search of society. For two days he saw nothing; upon the third day at sunset he met a beaver, who spoke to him, saying, "Who are you? whence do you come from? whither are you going?"

The Red-skin answered, "The great Spirit is my Father; He gave me all the earth, with its rivers and lakes, with the animals roaming through its prairies and forests; He gave me the birds flying in the air, and the fishes swimming in the sea."

The Beaver, surprised and irritated by so much insolence and presumption, commanded silence, and ordered the Red-skin to quit his domain immediately. A prolonged quarrel forthwith commenced between the Man and the Beaver, who defended his rights. The Beaver's only daughter, frightened at the noise, quitted her house, and stood between the irritated man and her father, entreating them by mild and conciliatory words to stop their quarrel. As the snow melts under the sun's rays, so at the voice and entreating look of the young child, the wrath of the stranger and his adversary gave place to a profound and lasting friendship —they embraced affectionately.

To render the union more durable, the Man asked the Beaver's daughter for his wife. After a few moments of deep thought, the latter presented her to him, saying, "It is the decree of the Great Spirit; I cannot oppose it ; take my daughter, cherish and protect her ; go in peace." The man and his wife continued their voyage to the mouth of the river.

At the entrance to a Prairie enamelled with gorgeous flowers, shut in with luxuriant fruit-bearing trees, in the midst of animals and birds, he built his wigwam. From this union sprang the Lenni-Lenapi, *i.e.*, the primitive family—known now as Delawares—a name given them by the whites—possibly derived from Lord Delaware, one of the early English Colonial Governors. Originally the Delawares resided in the great country west of the Mississippi. With the "Five Nations," well renowned in the Indian History of the vast American Continent, they seized and occupied a large territory south-east of their ancient domain.

Gradually they split up into three great tribes— "The Tortoise," "The Turkey," and "The Wolf." tribes.

In Penn's time they occupied the whole of Pennsylvania, and their possessions extended from the Potomac to the Hudson. As the whites increased the Delawares plunged deeper into the forests and yielded up their lands to the conquerors ; establishing themselves in Ohio on the margin of the Muskingum, whilst some of the tribes regained the shores and forests of the Mississippi. Government granted these Indians a small territory south-west of Fort Leavenworth, on the Missouri. In 1854 they ceded this territory.

The Lenni-Lenapi believe in the existence of two

Great Spirits—one they call Waka-Tanka, and the other Waka-Cheeka, *i.e.*, the Good Spirit, and the Bad Spirit; to these all the Manitous (or inferior Spirits), whether good or bad, must render homage and obedience.

These Indians also believe in a future state. It consists in a place of pleasure and repose, where the prudent in council, intrepid and courageous warriors, unwearied hunters, and men good and hospitable will obtain a lasting recompense.

For the *forkéd tongues* (liars), also for the slothful and indolent, there is a place of horrors. The first place is called Wak-an-da (country of life). The second place, Yoon-i-un-guch (insatiable gulf which never gives up its prey).

The "country of life" is an island vast in extent, and of ravishing and untold beauty. A lofty mountain rises in the centre of the island, and there upon the summit of his mountain-throne dwells the Great Spirit. There he overlooks his vast domain. He traces the interminable threadings of a thousand rivers, clear as crystal, which adorn its shady forests and flower-enamelled plains. He gazes down into the still deep lakes, which reflect for ever the glorious sun. Birds of brilliant plumage make the forests echo and re-echo again with sweetest melodies. All noble animals—buffaloes, elks, deer, goats and bighorns—graze peaceably in these laughing prairies. The lakes are never agitated by wind or tempest. Mire and slime never mingle with the limpid waters of the rivers.

Aquatic birds, otters, beavers, and fishes abound in them. Eternal spring reigns. Souls admitted into this realm regain their strength, and are free from all diseases. They experience no fatigue in hunting, and have no need of sleep or rest.

The Yoon-i-un-guch, on the other hand, environing "the country of life," is a broad, deep water, presenting an endless succession of cataracts and yawning gulfs, in which the roaring of the waves is frightful. On the summit of a rugged rock, which rises for ever above the wildest and angriest waves, dwells the Spirit of Evil. A fox lying in wait, a vulture ready to dart upon its prey. Waka-Cheeka watches the passage of souls to "the country of life." This passage is so narrow that only one soul at a time can possibly cross the bridge. The Bad Spirit presents himself in most hideous forms, and attacks each soul in turn. The cowardly, indolent soul immediately prepares for flight. Waka-Cheeka seizes it, and throws it into the open gulf, which never yields up its victim.

Another version says the Great Spirit has suspended a bunch of beautiful red bay bérries in the middle of the bridge, to try the virtue of those who cross it in their voyage to the "country of life." The Indian who has been active, and indefatigable in hunting, or victorious in war, avoids the tempting fruit. On the contrary, indolent and cowardly souls, tempted by the fascinating bays, stop and stretch out their hands to reach it; instantly the timbers composing the bridge sink heavily beneath them, and they are lost for ever in the abyss. The Lenni-Lenapi believe that the existence of good and evil spirits dates back to so remote an epoch that it is impossible for man to conceive its commencement; these spirits arc immutable, and death has no empire over them. These spirits of good and evil created the Manitous, or inferior spirits, who also enjoy immortality. All earthly blessings are attributed to the Good Spirit ; light and heat, health, the various productions of nature, and success on the war trail, and in the hunting grounds. From the Wicked Spirit comes contradiction and misfortunes, darkness, cold and hunger, failure on the war trail and in the hunting grounds, thirst, sickness, old age and death.

The poor Manitous cannot of themselves do good or evil; they are but mediators of the Great Spirits for the execution of their orders. They believe the soul to be material, although invisible and immortal ; it does not quit the body immediately after death, but that these two parts of men descend into the grave together, united during several days, sometimes during weeks and months. The soul having left the tomb, retards still its departure, being incapable of breaking the bonds which so intimately allied it to the body on earth. On account of this intimate union between the body and the soul, the Indians so carefully paint and adorn the body before burying it, and also place provisions, arms, and other utensils in the tomb. Many Indians place a favourite dish on the tomb of their relations during one month, convinced each time the food disappears that the soul of the departed has accepted the offering.

It is impossible any one should read these lines without noticing the striking points of resemblance with several traditions of Religion. In these Indian Religions are ideas of Creation, the terrestrial Paradise, Heaven and Hell, Angels and Demons.

CHAPTER XXVII.

"Lo ! how all things fade and perish !
From the memory of the old men
Fade away the great traditions,
The achievements of the Warriors,
The adventures of the Hunters,
All the wisdom of the Medas,*
All the craft of the Wabenos."†—*Longfellow.*

SACRIFICE TO WAKA-TANKA AND TO WAKA-CHEEKA.

MOST Indians offer two kinds of sacrifices. The Lenni-Lenapi also offer sacrifice to Waka-Tanka and Waka-Cheeka ; one to the good, and one to the evil spirit.

Of these ceremonies one is *general*, that of Waka-Tanka ; one is *particular*, that of Waka-Cheeka.

With all that Indiandom can give of solemnity is the great sacrifice of Waka-Tanka celebrated in the early spring of the year. It is made to obtain a blessing on the entire Nation, that the earth may be fruitful, that the hunting grounds may abound with beast and bird, that the rivers and lakes may be crowded with fish.

---

* Medas, Medicine Men.   † Wabeno, a Magician, a Juggler.

14

Before this great annual sacrifice the Chief calls together his Council, composed of inferior Chiefs, senior Warriors (who must have taken scalps in war), and the Medicine Men.

Their decision as to the proper time and place for the sacrifice is announced to the tribe by an Orator; then every one, without exception, commences to prepare himself to assist worthily at the festival, and give *éclat* to the ceremonies. Ten days before the celebration the principal Jugglers, who have the arrangement of the ceremonies, blacken their foreheads with a composition made from powdered charcoal and grease, as a token of mourning and penance. They retire then, either to their own wigwams or lodges, or otherwise into the most inaccessible thickets of the neighbouring forests. Here, alone, they pass their time in silence, in juggleries and practices of superstition; they observe a rigorous fast; and, at the least, pass ten days in complete abstinence—partaking of no nourishment.

In the meanwhile the medicine lodge is extended to its widest dimensions; all contribute to its decoration whatever they possess of value.

The day is named. In the early light of morning the Chiefs, followed by the Medicine Men and all the people, in full costume, painted carefully with brilliant colors, march in stately, savage procession to the lodge, and participate in a religious banquet, hastily prepared. During this repast, orators make speeches concerning the events of the past year—upon the successes or misfortunes of the Tribe.

The banquet ended, a large fire is kindled in the centre of the lodge. Twelve stones, each one weighing three pounds, are placed before the fire and made red-hot. *The victim*, which is *a white dog*, is presented to the jugglers by the great Chief, accompanied by his counsellors. The Sacrificant attaches the dog to the medicine-post, consecrated to this use and painted red. After making many supplications to Waka-Tanka, he despatches the victim with a single blow, tears out the heart, and divides it into three equal parts. They now draw out from the fire the twelve red-hot stones, and arrange them in three heaps, on each of which the Sacrificant places a piece of the heart, enveloped in Sumac leaves. Whilst these pieces are consuming, the jugglers raise with one hand their idols, and holding in the other a gourd filled with little stones, they beat the measure ; and dancing, surround the smoking sacrifice, at the same time imploring Waka-Tanka to grant a full share of blessings. When the heart and the leaves are entirely consumed, the ashes are collected in a beautiful doe-skin, ornamented with beads and embroidered with porcupine quills, and are thus presented to the Sacrificant, who goes forth from the lodge, preceded by four Masters of Ceremonies bearing the skin, and followed by the whole band of Medicine Men. After addressing the multitude, he divides the ashes of the sacrifice into six portions. Standing in a picturesque attitude, he casts the first towards Heaven, entreating the Good Spirit to grant his blessing ; the second he spreads on the Earth, to obtain an abundance of fruits and roots; the remaining portions are offered to the four cardinal points. To the East because the light of day, the sun, is given to them; to the West, because of showers which fertilize the plains and forests, and supply with water the springs, rivers, and lakes, from whence come the fish; to the North, because the snows and ice facilitate the operations of the chase; to the South, because southern gales call into life the new verdure, and then the animals bring forth their young. Lastly the Sacrificant implores all the elements to be propitious.

The Medicine Men are now thanked for all they have done to obtain the help and favour of Waka-Tanka during the coming year. The whole Tribe joyfully shout forth their approbation and withdraw to their wigwams to feast and dance. The white dog is carefully prepared and cooked, the whole confraternity of Medicine-Men receiving a portion in a wooden dish.

The difference between particular and general sacrifices consists in this: the heart of any one animal may be offered to the Good Spirit by one juggler only, in presence of one individual, or one or more families, in favour of whom the offering is made.

When any misfortune comes to a family, they immediately address the Chief of the jugglers, telling him their troubles; this communication is made most submissively, in order to obtain his intercession. He invites three amongst the initiated to deliberate on the affair. After many incantations the Chief rises, and makes known the causes of the anger of Waka-Cheeka. They proceed to the Lodge of Sacrifice, kindle a huge fire in it, and continue according to the Ritual of the Grand Sacrifice. The medicine men render themselves as hideous as possible, painting their faces and bodies, and wearing the most fantastical dresses, endeavouring to resemble exteriorly the Evil Spirit whom they serve. The supplicants now come into the lodge, and present the entrails of a cow by way of offering, placing themselves opposite the Medicine-Men. The red-hot stones, mounted in one heap, consume the entrails wrapped in sumac leaves. The Chief draws from his medicine sack secretly a bear's tooth, and hides it in his mouth ; covering his right eye with his hand, moaning and shrieking, and throwing his body into horrible contortions, such as become a lost soul entered already upon un-ending suffering, he, with an agility almost impossible to follow, pretends to draw from his eye the tooth of the bear already hidden in his mouth.

With a fiendish look of triumph he presents it to his too credulous clients, telling them the wrath of Waka-Cheeka is appeased. Several horses are then given to the juggler, and other merchandise of value amongst the Tribe. And, poor deluded people, they leave the place of Sacrifice joyous and content.

The time has come, dear Reader, for us to say good-bye. For a moment we seem to stand again, as we English explorers of that Western Prairie life stood, awaiting upon the departure platform of the little Mission Station the train that was to separate us from that Western World.

Like friends passing one another in Express Trains, we have but caught a glimpse of each other : our routes lie in different directions, and with regret we part, although we have so much still left unsaid. But if you find as much interest in reading as we did in studying Prairie life, we shall wring each other's hands as heartily in saying Good-bye, as many of those Western Ranchemen wrung ours thousands of miles away upon the Western Prairies.

And now, book, go forth, bearing upon thy pages these gleanings of Prairie life. Like all gleanings, thou art imperfect and be-drabbled. Imperfectly are thy chapters bound into a sheaf, in which I trace the silver thread of life ; the crimson of poured out blood — yea, and the blackened foot of death, has passed over thee ; yet, still I ask thee to perform thy work, and to come back to me in after years, *portantes manipulos tuos*, bringing thy sheaves with thee.

THE END.